STOP VULTURE FUND LAWSUITS

A HANDBOOK

Devi Sookun

COMMONWEALTH SECRETARIAT

Commonwealth Secretariat
Marlborough House, Pall Mall
London SW1Y 5HX, United Kingdom

© Commonwealth Secretariat 2010

All rights reserved. No part of this publication may be reproduced, stored in a retrieval system, or transmitted in any form or by any means, electronic or mechanical, including photocopying, recording or otherwise without the permission of the publisher.

Published by the Commonwealth Secretariat
Edited by Catherine Atthill
Designed by Wayzgoose
Cover design by Tattersall Hammarling & Silk
Printed by Hobbs the Printers Ltd, Totton, Hampshire

Views and opinions expressed in this publication are the responsibility of the author and should in no way be attributed to the institutions to which she is affiliated or to the Commonwealth Secretariat.

Wherever possible, the Commonwealth Secretariat uses paper sourced from sustainable forests or from sources that minimise a destructive impact on the environment.

Copies of this publication may be obtained from

The Publications Section
Commonwealth Secretariat, Marlborough House
Pall Mall, London SW1Y 5HX
United Kingdom
Tel: +44 (0)20 7747 6534
Fax: +44 (0)20 7839 9081
Email: publications@commonwealth.int
Web: www.thecommonwealth.org/publications

A catalogue record for this publication is available from the British Library.

ISBN (paperback): 978-1-84929-008-1
ISBN (e-book): 978-1-84859-055-7

Venice. A public place

Shylock:

This kindness will I show.
Go with me to a notary, seal me there
Your single bond; and, in a merry sport,
If you repay me not on such a day,
In such a place, such sum or sums as are
Express'd in the condition, let the forfeit
Be nominated for an equal pound
Of your fair flesh, to be cut off and taken
In what part of your body pleaseth me.

Act I, Scene III, *The Merchant of Venice,*
William Shakespeare

*Dedicated to
all 'poor' countries, which may or may
not be subject to lawsuits by vulture funds*

About the author

Poornimah Devi Sookun is a practising Barrister at Law of the Republic of Mauritius. She worked in independent practice before joining the Ministry of Justice of Mauritius as a Public Prosecutor, where she has worked for five years. She has conducted cases on behalf of the Government of Mauritius in both criminal and civil litigation. She has appeared before all the courts of Mauritius, including the Supreme Court and its appellate jurisdiction, as well as revenue courts for tax and valuation matters.

Devi also holds a Master's degree in Law (LLM) from King's College, University of London and was ranked first in the Barristers vocational examinations organised by the Mauritian Council of Legal Education. She was awarded the Sir Raymond Hein Memorial Prize in 1999. In 2000, she was a Chevening scholar.

Devi has been working as a Resident Legal Adviser at the Legal and Constitutional Affairs Division of the Commonwealth Secretariat since September 2006. In the course of her work, she observed the lacuna in the event of lawsuits brought against indebted countries. She therefore put pen to paper with a view of removing the mystery surrounding vulture funds and the daunting process of lawsuits against sovereign governments, by way of this Handbook.

Author's acknowledgements

I would like to thank everyone who has helped in the writing of this Handbook and in particular:

- The Commonwealth Secretariat for coming up with the project of a one stop legal referral service to assist heavily indebted poor countries. In particular, I should like to pay tribute to the then Legal Adviser and Head of the Law Development Section, Cheryl Thompson-Barrow, and the directors of the Legal and Constitutional Affairs Division, Economic Affairs Division and Special Advisory Services Division of the Secretariat.

- All the organisations which supported the workshops conducted by the Commonwealth Secretariat Legal Debt Clinic, especially DLA Piper, One Essex Court, African Development Bank (AfDB), International Monetary Fund (IMF), Macroeconomic Financial Management Institute (MEFMI), Crown Agents and Pole-Dette.

With special thanks to:

Vikash P Teeluckdharry, LLB (Hons), LLM Corporate Law and Barrister of the Middle Temple, for his contribution to Chapter 4, Negotiation; Colin Seelig, Associate Director, Crown Agents, for his contribution to Chapter 5, Debt Management; Catherine Atthill for her immense help in editing; and Guy Bentham for his invaluable support throughout the publication process.

Last, but not least, to my powerful team Elaine Ogilvie, Florence Kireta and Tiffany Chan, who provided administrative support which enabled the Legal Debt Clinic workshops in 40 heavily indebted poor countries. By the same token, special mention is made of the participants attending the workshops, as highlighted in this Handbook.

Contents

Abbreviations and Acronyms	xii
Introduction	1
PART I Briefing	**5**
1 Vulture Funds	**7**
1.1 What is a vulture fund?	7
1.2 The rise of vulture funds	8
1.3 Legal rights of vulture funds	11
2 Loan Agreements	**13**
2.1 What is a loan agreement?	13
2.2 Structure of a loan agreement	15
2.3 Concepts under a loan agreement	16
3 Lawsuits	**25**
3.1 Legal defences available to a sovereign debtor	26
3.2 Legal arguments supporting vulture fund claims	34
3.3 Effects of lawsuits	40
PART II Actions and Responses	**49**
4 Negotiation	**51**
4.1 When is negotiation possible?	51
4.2 What is negotiation?	52
4.3 Negotiation methods	54
5 Debt Management	**63**
5.1 What is public debt management?	65
5.2 Why is public debt management important?	66

| 5.3 | How to achieve effective debt management | 67 |
| 5.4 | Identifying loans which are targets for vulture funds | 69 |

6	**Responding to Lawsuits**	**73**
6.1	Negotiation	74
6.2	Contractual terms	74
6.3	'Name and shame' campaigns	76
6.4	Legal support for sovereign debtors	79

| **PART III Challenges and Solutions** | | **85** |

7	**Legislation**	**87**
7.1	Belgian law (2008)	88
7.2	UK law (2010)	88
7.3	US law (2008 and 2009)	90
7.4	French law (2007)	91

8	**International Initiatives**	**93**
8.1	HIPC debt relief initiatives (1996)	93
8.2	Norway (1998)	94
8.3	G8 (2005)	96
8.4	The Paris Club Initiative (2007)	96
8.5	China (2007)	97
8.6	Jubilee Debt Campaign	98

9	**Ways Forward**	**99**
9.1	International framework for restructuring sovereign debt	100
9.2	International arbitration court	100
9.3	Regulatory framework for public financial management	101

| **10** | **Conclusion** | **105** |

| **Bibliography** | | **111** |

| **List of Cases** | | **114** |

Annex 1. US Court Judgment in *FG Hemisphere Associates, LLC v Democratic Republic of Congo and Société Nationale D'Electricité (S.N.E.L.)*   115

Annex 2. Belgian Legislation   118

Annex 3. The UK Debt Relief (Developing Countries) Act 2010   119

Abbreviations and Acronyms

AfDB	African Development Bank
BATNA	Best alternative to a negotiated agreement
BVI	British Virgin Islands
CAC	Collective action clause
CHMF	Commonwealth HIPC Ministerial Forum
CS-DRMS	Commonwealth Secretariat Debt Recording Management System
DMFAS	Debt Management Financial Analysis System
DR Congo	Democratic Republic of Congo
DRF	Debt Reduction Facility
DRI	Debt Relief International
FSIA	Foreign Sovereign Immunities Act
HIPC	Heavily indebted poor country
IBRD	International Bank for Reconstruction and Development
ICC	International Chamber of Commerce
ICSID	International Centre for Settlement of Investment Disputes
IDA	International Development Association
IFI	International financial institution
IMF	International Monetary Fund
JDC	Jubilee Debt Campaign
LDC	Least developed country
MDG	Millennium development goal
MDRI	Multilateral Debt Relief Initiative
MEFMI	Macroeconomic Financial Management Institute
NGO	Non-governmental organisation
NPC	Negative pledge clause
ODA	Official development assistance
SDRM	Sovereign Debt Restructuring Mechanism
UNCITRAL	United Nations Commission on International Trade Law
UNCTAD	United Nations Conference on Trade and Development
UNITAR	United Nations Institute for Training and Research
WAIFEM	West African Institute for Financial and Economic Management

Introduction

Until recently lawsuits against sovereign states were rare. In the past, sovereign states enjoyed immunity from litigation. However, this situation changed dramatically when countries began to borrow money and entered into loan agreements to raise capital for economic development and infrastructure. Borrowing became an attractive solution for the least developed countries (LDCs), and in many cases a necessity. But borrowing means repayment, and even for a sovereign state the obligations of a loan contract do not disappear. Creditors cannot be forced to negotiate restructuring or refinancing plans, or an alternative option to demanding repayment. They cannot be barred from taking the ultimate solution under a loan agreement – suing the sovereign state before a court of law.

Vulture funds are investment funds which buy up distressed sovereign debt at a low price and then sue to secure a high return. The term 'vulture fund' is a vivid image, which describes the way these funds prey on poor countries on the brink of debt relief. Such creditors do not hesitate to take legal action. As courts of law are bound to deal with a lawsuit according to the terms of the loan agreement, judgments have had a negative, often unfair, impact on sovereign debtors, at times paralysing their economies. From the point of view of the creditors, they have been acting legally, but they have been named and shamed as vultures, and branded as immoral and perverse. However, the question that arises is: should the principles of legal egalitarianism apply when the debtor is a poor country in debt distress, and where poverty and hunger prevail?

Lawsuits against sovereign debtors became more prominent after the International Monetary Fund (IMF) called on all creditors to write off the debts of heavily indebted poor countries (HIPCs). The international financial institutions (IFIs) introduced the HIPC Initiative in 1996 under pressure from millions of campaigners who believed that the burden of debt was undermining any prospect of development in some of the world's poorest countries. Progress has been slow, although the Initiative was enhanced in 1999. One reason has been that creditors are reluctant to participate in the Initiative and may choose to sell on their debts to vulture funds.

The Commonwealth Secretariat Legal Debt Clinic

By 2003 Commonwealth Heads of Government had recognised that the debt burden in developing member states was a major obstacle to developing key socio-economic sectors. They welcomed the advisory and consensus building work of the Commonwealth HIPC Ministerial Forum (CHMF) and encouraged its efforts to help heavily indebted poor countries achieve a sustainable exit from debt. At ministerial meetings, the Forum noted that debt-distressed countries were facing lawsuits from commercial and bilateral creditors that were hindering debt relief. The lawsuits were mostly taking place in foreign courts in places such as London, New York City and Paris, and the debtor countries needed legal advice to deal with the vulture funds. However, they did not have the resources to take action and could not afford to pay for legal advice from UK and US law firms. To meet this need, in 2006 the Forum set up a one stop legal referral service to assist countries that faced lawsuits, for an initial term of three years. This service is the Commonwealth Secretariat Legal Debt Clinic, originally known as the HIPC Clinic.

The Legal Debt Clinic's brief is to work with officials from ministries of both justice and finance, as vulture fund lawsuits involve both legal and debt management issues. It aims to encourage officials from the various ministries to work together, share understanding of the risks involved in loan agreements and identify actions that governments can take when they face lawsuits or the threat of lawsuits. It organises capacity-building workshops and on request provides advice for countries facing lawsuits. It has conducted four major capacity-building workshops for 11 Caribbean and 15 African countries. It has obtained collaboration and funding facilities from Pole-Dette and conducted a successful meeting for 16 indebted Francophone countries. The Clinic has assisted with capacity building and awareness-raising campaigns on the need to ensure that lawyers participate in the loan contract process. It has also been able to help countries negotiate and obtain withdrawal of lawsuits. It has successfully advocated for a change of legislation by the UK Government and has worked with the Jubilee Debt Campaign on the need for this legislation to stop further lawsuits under UK jurisdiction. In response, the UK Government has enacted the Debt Relief (Developing Countries) Act 2010.[1]

About the Handbook

This Handbook is based on the experiences of the Legal Debt Clinic over three years. It reflects the needs expressed by workshop participants from both legal and financial backgrounds for knowledge, understanding and expertise to enable them to work effectively and collaboratively. The Handbook is in three parts.

Part I, Briefing, covers the background needed to understand vulture funds. It highlights concepts and myths surrounding vulture funds' activities, especially lawsuits. As loan agreements are the basis of the funds' operations, it explains key concepts and clauses in loan agreements to help countries understand what is involved before and after signing an agreement. Finally, as there is little documented information about lawsuits against sovereign debtors, especially with regard to the legal aspects, it provides a compilation of landmark cases.

Part II, Actions and Responses, offers advice on actions which can be taken by sovereign debtors to avoid lawsuits or mitigate their effects. It highlights some practices to adopt, including negotiation at all stages, understanding of debt management practices and responsible borrowing, and identifying available options when faced with litigation.

Part III, Challenges and Solutions, describes the steps being taken at the international level in terms of legislation, arbitration and regulation to try to curb the activities of vulture funds. Vulture funds are aware of their strongly protected contractual legal rights which they can exploit through lawsuits. One of the best ways of curtailing this exploitation is legislation. Only a few countries have adopted this stand and these are highlighted here.

Using the Handbook

The Handbook is intended for both legal and financial officials, and others working in related areas, such as debt relief campaigners, non-governmental organisation (NGO) advisers, and students of finance and the law. It can be used in several ways: readers may read the Handbook straight through or they can choose the chapters most relevant to their needs to fill gaps in their knowledge or expertise. In addition, it can be used as a resource to brief colleagues from other disciplines or as a basis for seminars or workshops, as it follows the pattern of the Legal Debt Clinic's own workshops.

The Handbook aims to expose the often secretive operations of vulture funds, many of which are based in tax havens and have been set up with the sole purpose of pursuing debt in poor countries. It provides the background information needed to understand how the funds work and the lawsuits they engage in. It suggests actions and responses open to sovereign debtors to avoid these lawsuits and provides advice on how to respond to them when they arise. The Handbook also points to more far-reaching solutions. Responsible borrowing and adequate fiscal policies may pave the way for sovereign states to attain greater economic stability with less intervention by IFIs. At the international level, legislation, arbitration and a comprehensive code of conduct and a one stop regulatory body may be the way forward. Through this Handbook, the Legal Debt Clinic hopes to extend its work and share its experience with a wider audience, enabling them to take action. Above all, when the targets of the vulture funds are poor countries where people are living on less than a dollar a day, what is needed is for all those involved – creditors and debtors, governments and international institutions – to take moral responsibility for creating a better and fairer system.

PART I

Briefing

Part I of this Handbook covers the essential background needed for an understanding of vulture funds and the way they operate. This briefing supports the actions and responses described in Part II and underpins the more far-reaching solutions proposed in Part III.

Chapter 1, Vulture Funds, explains what vulture funds are, how they operate and their culture of litigation. It discusses their legality, and contrasts this with moral and ethical arguments against their exploitation of poor countries and debt relief initiatives.

Chapter 2, Loan Agreements, shows how these agreements are the basis of vulture funds' operations. The chapter explains key concepts and clauses which should be taken into account before and after signing an agreement to avoid leaving loopholes which the fund can exploit in court.

Chapter 3, Lawsuits, provides a compilation of landmark cases, showing how the concepts and clauses explained in Chapter 2 are applied in the courts. The cases illustrate how lawsuits can exploit debt relief initiatives. The chapter demonstrates how important it is to negotiate the original loan or settlement agreement with the utmost care.

CHAPTER 1

Vulture Funds

We particularly condemn the perversity where vulture funds purchase debt at a reduced price and make a profit from suing the debtor country to recover the full amount owed – a morally outrageous outcome.

Gordon Brown, speaking as UK Chancellor of the
Exchequer, at the United Nations in 2002[2]

The term 'vulture fund' describes how private investment firms and hedge funds prey on poor countries on the brink of debt relief – like vultures waiting to swoop down on a rotting carcase. This chapter defines vulture funds and their origins. It examines their culture and the legitimacy of their operations, to show why so many people condemn them.

1.1 What is a vulture fund?

Vulture funds are commercial creditors which buy up the debts of poor countries at a cheap rate and then sue them to secure a high return, which is the sole reason for their investment. Vulture funds have become increasingly retrogressive since they began impeding the progress of debt relief in many heavily indebted poor countries.

Market practitioners would probably prefer to describe the funds as 'distressed debt investors' and would regard the vulture metaphor as too harsh. However, in 2002 Gordon Brown (then UK Chancellor of the Exchequer and subsequently Prime Minister), speaking at the UN, described vulture funds as perverse and immoral. The reason for this is their shrewdness when it comes to profiting from the problems of a sovereign government.

The IMF has defined vulture funds as companies which buy the debt of poor nations cheaply when it is about to be written off and then sue for the full value of the debt plus interest – which may be ten times what they paid for it.[3] The key characteristics of a vulture fund are:

- It is not the primary lender of the money;

- It acquires the title deed of the debt through the purchase of the money owed on a secondary market; and

- It goes to court to sue the sovereign debtor for the full value of the debt, plus interest, generally making a profit of 3 to 20 times its investment.[4]

1.2 The rise of vulture funds

Sovereign states used to enjoy immunity from litigation. So how have vulture funds come to play their current role?

In 1996 the international financial institutions introduced the HIPC Initiative, with a call to all creditors to write off the debts of HIPCs. It has been argued that the leniency of this initiative gave rise to more lawsuits and highlighted the fact that litigation was the easiest way of obtaining a good return. But this is not the only reason for the rise of vulture funds. Investment in distressed funds as a lucrative business had been happening secretly for some time.

Historically, the major debt crisis of the 1980s in Latin America gave birth to the vulture fund operations which are now affecting almost every HIPC country around the world. What lay behind this? The reason for the rise of vulture funds was the mode of borrowing at that time. Borrowing by least developed countries used to be through syndicated banks, and not through bond lending as today. In the 1970s, commercial banks began to lend to developing countries directly. Commercial loans were an attractive and sophisticated form of borrowing. However, there were drawbacks, as commercial loans carried high interest rates, coupled with a variable rate that was passed on to the borrower.

Following the debt crisis of the 1980s, the US Federal Reserve began to tighten its monetary policy. This led to an increase in nominal interest rates. Borrowing countries were forced to repay at very high interest rates and the debt profiles of many borrowing countries became unsustainable. Restructuring measures were brought in to mitigate these problems of huge indebtedness. From 1982 to 1989 there was a long period of restructuring sovereign debt. However, by 1989 it became clear that in spite of these measures the Latin American states' financial position was not improving.

The debt restructuring process that then took place, known as the Baker Plan, was not successful. The rescheduling of loans between banks and sovereign debtors became a more complex issue than had been predicted. The banks foresaw an endless cycle of rescheduling and debtor countries began to tire of the process.

In March 1989, US Treasury Secretary Nicholas Brady designed the Brady Plan in an attempt to address the debt crisis. Under the Plan, loans were exchanged for sovereign bonds that could be freely traded. By 1998 it was evident that sovereign debt had been converted from syndicated bank loans to securitised bonds. Brady bonds became a generic term for bonds issued during sovereign debt restructuring, but they referred specifically to the exchange of commercial bank loans for bond instruments.

These bonds were offered to the public and the proceeds of the bond offering were used to repay the borrowing country's outstanding bank loan indebtedness. However, with the creation of the sovereign bond market, non-bank investors began to hold substantial amounts of sovereign debt. This changed the dynamics of sovereign debt restructuring.

When commercial bank syndicated loans were unpaid, there was an orderly process for restructuring the loan in the case of indebtedness. The restructuring of the loan under the terms of the Brady Plan was done by the debtor country and an ad hoc committee of the largest institutional creditors, known as the Bank Advisory Committee. The latter would commit to restructuring on agreed terms. The bank would undertake to roll over the debt to avoid declaring default on the debt on its balance sheet. It also indirectly helped the country's economy to perform better, which kept the borrowing country tied to the bank in the long term. However, other creditors were under no obligation to accept these terms.

Despite their advantages, the Brady bond restructurings undermined the orderly restructuring process. They also broadened the base of investors. Such investors, with their divergent interests, grew in number and became increasingly difficult to manage. Large banking institutions are often interested in ensuring that developing countries commit to IMF-approved economic policies as a condition of obtaining finance or refinance. However, small hedge funds and smaller investors have a different approach. They also find it much easier to break away from the group and ask for immediate repayment. This means there are fewer factors to deter vulture funds from purchasing the defaulted debt when it is about to be written off by the primary lender, or when a restructuring plan is ongoing between the primary lender and the sovereign debtor.

Vulture funds became prominent in the mid-1990s. They were first introduced by the US-based billionaire Paul Singer, who runs the biggest vulture fund, known as Elliott Associates. In 1996, Elliott spent almost US$12m on the purchase of 'distressed' Peruvian debt and four years later forced Peru to pay over US$55m to redeem it. Singer is reputedly worth £8bn.[5]

Elliott Associates' success in *Elliott Associates, LP v Banco de la Nacion and The Republic of Peru*[6] (see Chapter 3, Lawsuits) shifted power to the vulture fund creditors.

By holding out in Peru's debt restructuring process, Elliott Associates successfully sued and claimed the full amount owed, with interest and costs. Peru had to settle by paying Elliott Associates US$56.3m for a debt originally worth US$11.4m, so that it could restructure with the other creditors. Other investors found this mode of operation extremely profitable.

This case proved that the actions of the vulture funds are very profitable. It gave rise to the actions of many other vulture funds that threaten most of the distressed sovereign states in today's world.

According to the IMF, litigating creditors are concentrated in the USA and UK, and in the UK protectorate tax haven, the British Virgin Islands (BVI).[7] Another vulture fund, Kensington International Ltd, based in the Cayman Islands, sued the Democratic Republic of Congo (DR Congo) for US$30m in the High Court in London. A more recent vulture fund case was brought against the Republic of Zambia by Michael Sheehan, Director of Donegal International Ltd, which is based in BVI (see Chapter 3, Lawsuits, for further details).

These examples of how the funds undertake aggressive litigation after purchasing debt at huge discounts illustrate the litigious culture of the vulture funds. In the interests of sovereign states, litigation should not be the first option, but rather a last resort to be avoided at all costs. Sovereign debtors need to be aware of the underlying litigious culture of vulture funds and be prepared to take alternative steps (for example those discussed in Part II, Actions and Responses).

Several campaigning groups have lobbied energetically for debt relief. The Jubilee Debt Campaign is one such group that campaigned against the actions of Donegal International Ltd after it sued Zambia in 2007. The UK Government acknowledged the work of the campaigners, releasing a press statement in which, for the first time, the damaging effects of lawsuits were recognised.[8] The Jubilee Debt Campaign has also called for UK legislation to stop lawsuits being brought by vulture funds.

Another effective campaign has been through two BBC *Newsnight* programmes featuring the journalist Greg Palast. Palast tried to obtain interviews with vulture fund owners about their litigious actions. The first programme was in February 2007, after Donegal International Ltd won its case against the Republic of Zambia. The second was in February 2010, after the vulture funds Hamsah Investments and Wall Capital Ltd won their case against Liberia. Both these broadcasts are available at Greg Palast's website.[9]

amazon.co.uk

Thank you for shopping at Amazon.co.uk!

Invoice for
Your order of 24 May, 2013
Order ID 202-7868059-5420319
Invoice number DpLXZmhQN
Invoice date 24 May, 2013

Billing Address
Sebastian Perry
106 Palace Road
Flat D
LONDON SW2 3JZ
United Kingdom

Shipping Address
Sebastian Perry
106 Palace Road
Flat D
LONDON SW2 3JZ
United Kingdom

1 A2

Qty.	Item	Our Price (excl. VAT)	VAT Rate	Total Price
1	**Stop Vulture Fund Lawsuits: A Handbook** Paperback. Sookun, Devi. 184929008 (** P-1-F5BC154 **)	£14.30	0%	£14.30

Shipping charges		£0.00
Subtotal (excl. VAT) 0%		£14.30
Total VAT		£0.00
Total		£14.30

Conversion rate - £1.00 : EUR 1.17

This shipment completes your order.

You can always check the status of your orders or change your account details from the 'Your Account' link at the top of each page on our site.

Thinking of returning an item? PLEASE USE OUR ON-LINE RETURNS SUPPORT CENTRE.

Our Returns Support Centre (www.amazon.co.uk/returns-support) will guide you through our Returns Policy and provide you with a printable personalised return label. Please have your order number ready (you can find it next to your order summary, above). Our Returns Policy does not affect your statutory rights.

Amazon EU S.a.r.l, 5 Rue Plaetis, L-2338, Luxembourg
VAT number : GB727255821

Please note - this is not a returns address - for returns - please see above for details of our online returns centre

0/DQPwZZh6N/-1 of 1-//2ND_LETTER/econ-uk/6917791/0528-16:45/0525-15:19 Pack Type : A2

1.3 Legal rights of vulture funds

Vulture funds are usually secondary owners of a debt. As secondary owners they have a lawful right to repayment. This is similar to the undisputed right of the primary lender who originally lent the money to the sovereign debtor fulfilling all necessary legal requirements. The vulture fund creditor takes over the rights of the primary lender through the purchase of the debt, since a debt can be traded as a property right and can be validly sold or purchased.

A pertinent question that has been raised at Commonwealth Secretariat Legal Debt Clinic seminars is whether a debt that is purchased or assigned is still valid. If a debt is purchased on the secondary market or has been validly assigned, even at a much discounted rate, the legal claim nevertheless remains valid. This has been confirmed by a judgment in the case of *Pravin Banker Associates Ltd v Banco Popular del Peru* (1997),[10] where the court ruled that the claim of this vulture fund was valid and enforceable.

In the most recent case of *Donegal International Ltd v Republic of Zambia & Anor*[11] (see Chapter 3, Lawsuits), the judge noted that although Donegal was deliberately withholding documents and although he had to order Donegal to disclose them, its actions were not strictly speaking illegal. Again, a valid judgment was given in favour of Donegal. So even if the vulture fund's activities can be described as immoral – as many people in Zambia are living on less than a dollar a day – Donegal had a legal right to its claim. This example highlights the fact that in any discussion of vulture funds there may, on the one hand, be moral arguments and, on the other, legal and financial arguments, so that the discussion takes place on two different levels.

In an interview with Greg Palast on the BBC *Newsnight* programme,[12] the director of Donegal, Michael Sheehan, responded as follows:

> Greg Palast: *Aren't you just profiteering from the work of good people who are trying to save lives by cutting the debt of these poor nations?*
>
> Michael Sheehan: *Well there was a proposal for investment. That's all I can talk about right now.*

In their defence, the vulture funds claim that they function as distressed debt funds, which are a necessity on the financial market. The funds argue that they allow private sector lenders to advance further loans to HIPC countries although they know that the sovereign country may default in the future. Big institutional investors do not like suing sovereign countries and therefore can obtain some return by selling their defaulted debt to vulture funds. Thus it can be argued that the presence of vulture funds is essential in economic terms.

Conclusion

This chapter has explained what vulture funds are, how they came into being and the way they operate, including an assessment of the legality of their actions. It has touched on several important legal cases and concepts which will be discussed more fully in later chapters. Vulture funds have a valid right to their title when indebted countries fail in their legal obligations under their contractual loan agreement. Nevertheless, there has been increasing recognition, including by some courts, that HIPC countries should be helped to resolve their unsustainable debt. The prime aim of the whole mechanism of debt relief through debt restructuring and the HIPC Initiative has been to help heavily indebted countries to come out of unsustainable debt. Only successful debt relief will allow an equal distribution of economic resources and help indebted countries embark on a path towards sustainable development. Chapter 7, Legislation, and Chapter 8, International Initiatives, highlight international action to write off debt. When there is such a concerted international effort, can it be right for the vulture funds to benefit from debt relief?

Two key lessons emerge from this chapter:

- Sovereign debtors need to be aware of the underlying litigious culture of vulture funds and be prepared to take alternative remedies (see Part II, Actions and Responses);
- The actions of the vulture funds, though unethical, unfair and exploitative, remain legal.

Further reading

- Meirion Jones, 'Vulture Fund Threat to Third World – How Corporations Continue to Rape the World's Poor', BBC *Newsnight*, 14 February 2007, available at http://www.informationclearinghouse.info/article17070.htm
- Jubilee Debt Campaign, http://www.jubileedebtcampaign.org.uk/
- Greg Palast, http://www.gregpalast.com
- Felix Salmon, 'In Defense of Vulture Funds', Saturday, 24 February 2007, http://www.felixsalmon.com/000667.html
- Ian Vásquez, 'The Brady Plan and Market Based Solutions to Debt Crisis', *The Cato Journal*, No. 16, Vol. 2, http://www.cato.org/pubs/journal/cj16n2-4.html

CHAPTER 2

Loan Agreements

If you repay me not on such a day ... Be nominated for an equal pound of your fair flesh, to be cut off and taken in what part of your body pleaseth me.

William Shakespeare, *The Merchant of Venice*

Vulture funds are successful because courts enforce their right to collect the full value of a debt as stipulated in the loan agreement. Nearly all the arguments used to justify enforcement of the funds' rights are found in the different clauses of the agreement entered into when the loan is assigned from the primary lender to the vulture fund.

This chapter explains what a loan agreement is and outlines the main types of agreement. It describes their basic structure, and summarises the main concepts and clauses of a typical loan agreement and some of the loopholes which allow vulture funds to operate.

Finally, it stresses the importance of understanding what a loan agreement and its clauses entail, and draws lessons from various cases and experiences.

2.1 What is a loan agreement?

A loan agreement is the written contract between a creditor and a borrower. It sets out the rights and obligations of each party regarding a specified loan. The agreement defines the following:

- the parties to the contract;
- the purpose for which the obligations of both parties are being drafted; and
- the terms and conditions on which the agreement is valid.

In a normal contract between two parties only the intentions of the parties involved in the process are noted down in the agreement. However, in a loan agreement, the concerns of other creditors may have a role in the agreement between one particular creditor and the sovereign debtor.

In the present context, a loan agreement is a legally binding contract which makes a specific value of funds available for disbursement to a borrower by a particular lender. The loan agreement also stipulates in its clauses the amount to be disbursed in accordance with the terms set out in a repayment schedule or a promissory note.

Every loan agreement has unique features which depend on the purpose of the loan. Every agreement contains some basic provisions. Some agreements are used as 'standard' contracts. Regional Development Banks or IFIs such as the IMF, World Bank and African Development Bank (AfDB) use a standard contract. The reason for this is to safeguard the interests of the creditor, since the borrower has no say in terms and conditions already drafted. It also brings a degree of consistency to all lending and ensures that there are not different rules for different borrowers. There will also be a second agreement with other clauses highlighting the terms and conditions under which the project will be fulfilled, known as a project specific agreement or project specific contractual terms.

However, since the standard contract is known to be non-negotiable and is drafted after taking into account the lender's concerns about the risk of non-payment, it is always advisable for the borrower to have a proper understanding of all the terms included in the standard agreement. An example of such a loan agreement can be obtained from the AfDB website.[13]

General advice given by the Legal Debt Clinic is that it is always worth reading through and challenging the precise way the standard clauses are formulated, even though they appear to be non-negotiable.

The nature and form of loan agreement will differ according to the status of the creditor. IFIs will have one type of loan agreement, bilateral creditors another and commercial creditors yet another. Assigned new creditors, in other words vulture funds, usually enter into an agreement known as a settlement agreement which is attached to the initial loan agreement.

This chapter focuses on the structure of a loan agreement where the contract does not have standard non-negotiable terms and conditions. These are the contracts that are the subject of lawsuits and are therefore particularly relevant for vulture funds.

In every loan agreement, the terms and conditions can be classified under three categories of clauses:

A   Operational clauses

B   Protective clauses

C   Change of circumstance clauses

Operational clauses make the loan agreement workable, that is they highlight the amount being disbursed, the purpose of the agreement and how the repayment will be scheduled.

Protective clauses enable the creditor to maximise its security by imposing conditions on the borrower. They limit the future activity and freedom of the borrower and will be analysed below.

Change of circumstance clauses aim to deal with problems which may arise during the course of the loan agreement, as predicted in the operational clauses, or they may cover events which can be envisaged and may happen outside the control of any of the parties to the contract. Such events are known as 'events of default'. There may be many of these, but they have to be specifically provided for under the contract.

2.2 Structure of a loan agreement

The basic structure of a loan agreement is as follows:

- **The preamble** stipulates the broad intentions of the parties; it is advisable to widen it to include several intentions.

- **The definition section** defines fundamental concepts used in the contract; it defines the role of the people who will represent each party and defines terms such as 'floating rate of interest', 'the project' and 'the currency'.

- **The description** describes the project, the parties' obligations and any time limit for the fulfilment of the obligations.

- **Terms of repayment** stipulate the currency, interest rates and period of the loan.

- **Default clauses** describe events which will be considered as a failure to fulfil the obligations under the contract and what the consequences and penalty will be.

- **Legal provisions** set out the governing law of the contract and the means of obtaining redress if one of the parties defaults on their obligations under the contract.

- **Clauses of conditions precedent** make disbursement possible or make the contract effective in terms of grants.

This is the structure of a standard contract that any creditor will try to make a sovereign debtor agree and adhere to.

2.3 Concepts under a loan agreement

We now highlight some important concepts and clauses which throw light on how vulture funds operate. We give an overview of these concepts, rather than a detailed analysis. Most of them will be illustrated by cases and examples in later chapters. The concepts are:

A   Operational clauses
  Applicable law clause

B   Protective clauses
  Conditions precedent
  Negative pledge clauses (NPCs)
  Pari passu clauses
  Collective action clauses (CACs)

C   Change of circumstance clauses
  Events of default clauses
  Late payment of amounts due
  Breach of obligations
  Misrepresentation and warranty
  Cross default
  Material adverse change default

A   Operational clauses

Applicable law clause

The most important and relevant operational clause for the purposes of lawsuits is the applicable law clause.

This provides for the applicable law which will govern the loan agreement in the case of disagreement between the parties or default in their obligations. Usually, both parties determine the applicable law. Parties tend to opt for a sufficiently developed jurisdiction: the UK or New York jurisdictions have been favourites. The borrower should always opt for a jurisdiction where it will be equally protected in its rights. With the development of future legislation regulating the activities of the vulture funds (as in the UK and USA), it is advisable to opt for one of these countries as applicable law. At the time of writing, the UK has passed legislation regulating the activities of vulture funds and the USA has reintroduced a Bill relating to stopping vulture funds' activities. (There is more about this in Chapter 7, Legislation.)

It is a mistake for the sovereign debtor to submit to a jurisdiction not provided for in the loan agreement. Refusing to submit is a powerful legal argument against the creditor which will undoubtedly lead to the withdrawal of the lawsuit.

In the case of *Donegal International Ltd v Republic of Zambia & Anor*,[14] Zambia submitted to the UK jurisdiction, whereas Donegal was unsuccessful in the Cayman Islands and British Virgin Islands. If Zambia had not submitted to the UK jurisdiction, the vulture fund would not have had recourse to court until Zambia expressly waived its right before the UK court during court proceedings.

The Legal Debt Clinic encountered another bilateral agreement which involved an African government as the borrower and a Yugoslavian company as the lender. The applicable law governing the contract was that of Switzerland. The settlement of disputes was to be referred to arbitration by the International Chamber of Commerce, Paris, in accordance with its rules of procedure. Arbitration was to take place in London, UK, or any other place mutually agreed by the parties. This example shows how the borrower exposed itself to an unknown law, Swiss law, and to settlement in a foreign jurisdiction.

B Protective clauses

Conditions precedent

Conditions precedent are preconditions which must be fulfilled before a loan agreement becomes operational. Once funds are lent by a creditor, it becomes proof of the fact that the conditions precedent have been met. Every loan agreement, whether with an international financial institution or any other creditor, has conditions precedent. Such conditions relate either to the validity of the contract or to the disbursement of funds by the creditor. Until the conditions are met there is no exchange of obligations by either party. In some cases, there are time limits to fulfil the conditions precedent and it may be difficult to honour these. It is worth seeing if these time limits can be removed: otherwise it is essential to keep to them.

It is always advisable to obtain a legal opinion about the conditions precedent before signing an agreement. The clause on conditions precedent varies but will usually contain the following words: 'This loan agreement shall not become effective until ...' or 'No disbursement of funds will be made until ... '.

The conditions precedent may vary from one creditor to another. Debtors should always pay attention to them as they may have an important impact if the matter goes to court and they had an obligation to fulfil under the contract. This is particularly relevant when the conditions precedent concern such legal issues as requirements which will make the contract valid and enforceable, warranty issues or who has the power to enter the agreement and bind the government. It must be stressed that the conditions precedent have important implications regarding the validity of loan agreements and so are most carefully drafted and presented by the creditor.

Borrowers need to be cautious, as legal implications and liability will follow once the conditions are met. It is advisable to make a list of documents required under the conditions precedent and to include the list in the contract so as not to fall into default. Usually the vulture fund will also include certain conditions precedent after stepping into the rights of the original creditor in the settlement agreement.

Negative pledge clauses

Negative pledge clauses are standard provisions in loan instruments which regulate the granting of security interests in a sovereign debtor's assets. They are categorised as protective clauses in the loan agreement.

NPCs may prohibit borrowers from encumbering their assets through the creation of liens, mortgages or other encumbrances, or they may require borrowers who do encumber their assets to secure a creditor's claim equally and rateably in order not to subordinate the present creditor's claim to those of prior creditors. The purpose of such an NPC is to preserve the assets and future revenues of borrowers by preventing the assets from being used to secure other loans which would jeopardise their current priority claim on the sovereign's assets. It is also referred to as a 'covenant of equal coverage'.

An NPC gives the creditor security. The borrower should negotiate this clause as a reason to borrow money at a lower interest rate or to obtain other financial advantages.

> **An example from the African Development Bank's agreement**
>
> It is the policy of the Bank, in making loans to, or with the guarantee of, its Member States not to seek, in normal circumstances, special security from the Member State concerned. However, the Borrower or the Guarantor shall ensure that no other External Debt shall have priority over its loan or guarantee obligation in the allocation, realization or distribution of foreign exchange held under the control or for the benefit of such Member State.

Pari passu *clauses*

A *pari passu* clause is included in every sovereign debt agreement. There has been much debate about this principle and its meaning, especially after the pronouncement by the Belgian courts, when it was raised by Elliott Associates.[15] The traditional meaning of *pari passu* clauses is that all creditors should treated equally in repayment terms in the event of bankruptcy or insolvency. The Belgian judgment introduced a new interpretation: that one creditor cannot receive any repayment until all other outstanding creditors receive a *pro rata* repayment. This clause prevented the sovereign debtor, Peru, pursuing its debt restructuring by withholding payment from Elliott Associates. This clause therefore stops debtor countries from agreeing to a settlement agreement or restructuring their debt with some creditors who are agreeable, and not take into account payment to the creditors who disagree. The power of this clause will be illustrated in Chapter 3, Lawsuits, by the case of *Elliott Associates, LP v Banco de la Nacion and The Republic of Peru*.

From the perspective of threats by vulture funds and their activities, the *pari passu* clause has become an effective means of seeking repayment if the creditor is unwilling to agree to a restructuring process. This was the strongest argument made in the case of Elliott Associates against Peru, which the Belgian court accepted. In law, Elliott Associates was right to object to the restructuring process and demand repayment of its debt on the basis of the *pari passu* clause.

For reference we provide an example of a *pari passu* clause in a loan agreement between Republic of Cameroon and Midland Bank PLC, where the latter subsequently sold the debt to Rumbold, a vulture fund. Such a clause can stand on its own as a paragraph or is inserted as part of a clause:

> Under paragraph 9 'Undertakings'
>
> 9.1 The Borrower undertakes with each of the Bank and the Agent that, from the date of this Agreement and so long as any moneys are owing under this Agreement, it will:
>
> (d) ensure that its obligations under this Agreement shall at all times rank at least *pari passu* with all its other present and future unsecured and unsubordinated obligations of the Issuer, present and future.

Collective action clauses

In order to reduce protracted sovereign debt restructuring it was necessary to find a clause in the contract which would allow swift and binding debt restructuring. CACs are clauses in bond agreements that allow the restructuring of a country's debt, as long as a majority of creditors approve. CACs weaken the power of vulture funds by eliminating the legal basis on which one vulture fund creditor can hold out and stop a debt restructuring process. CACs force all creditors to accept a restructuring decision approved by a sufficient majority. For example, in the Peru case, if there had been a CAC, Elliott Associates would have been forced to accept the debt restructuring agreement, as the majority of creditors were willing to restructure the debt. Elliott Associates would have had no legal basis for bringing the lawsuit as a hold-out creditor, or would not even have been allowed to hold out.

CACs provide a way of discouraging vulture funds, but they are used in bonds and not loan agreements. The G10 endorsed the use of CACs in 1996 and other states followed suit in 1998. IMF communiqués also call for increased use of CACs. After the success of the Elliott Associates lawsuit, one measure against the *pari passu* clause has been the CACs.

It is argued that although CACs can only be utilised in bonds, the principles and conditions provided for under CACs can be inserted as clauses in a loan agreement. However, the drawback is that such clauses are unattractive to many creditors and can effectively raise the costs of borrowing. The Legal Debt Clinic advises more prudent borrowing with safer clauses, even at the expense of high costs of borrowing. If all sovereign debtors insist on including such clauses, creditors will readily accept them.

C   Change of circumstance clauses

Note: This section uses the terms 'defaulting' and 'non-defaulting' party as well as 'borrower' and 'lender'.

Change of circumstance clauses are needed as protection by the non-defaulting party if the defaulting party fails to fulfil part of its obligation under a loan agreement. As the lender has already given money to the borrower under the agreement, change of circumstance clauses are often for the benefit of the lender, as it believes that the borrower is more likely to be in difficulty and be unable to repay on time. The lender therefore includes a set of circumstances which would make the borrower unable to escape its obligation. These changing sets of circumstances can be circumstances arising from those already defined in the loan agreement or new circumstances beyond the control of the parties. They are known as the events of default.

Events of default clauses

Events of default clauses allow the non-defaulting party to stop performing its obligations if such events occur on the part of the other party. They are critical clauses in a loan agreement. The events of default provisions are drafted taking into account the commercial realities of the transaction.

Events of default are those material circumstances which can substantially prejudice the position of the non-defaulting party. The agreement will set out the circumstances to be explicitly as considered events of default, which may even enable the non-defaulting party to terminate the agreement. The defaulting party will have to examine the background to see if the default clauses really will prejudice the non-defaulting party. Otherwise, the defaulting party may find itself in difficulties.

> **Clause of default in the settlement agreement entered between Zambia and Donegal International Ltd**
>
> Under the default sections, clauses 2.1, 2.2 and 2.3, it was provided that Zambia should make 36 monthly payments to Donegal in the total sum of US$14,781,498.96, together with interest on the unpaid balance calculated at the rate of 6 per cent per annum. It also provided that *only 21 days* after Zambia defaulted upon *any payment*, Donegal could elect to terminate the settlement agreement by a notice in writing.
>
> 'Upon service of the Notice, *this Agreement will be null and void* and of no effect and Donegal will be entitled to judgment in respect of the Debt in full with interest at 8 per cent per annum compounding quarterly having given credit for any amounts already received pursuant to Clause 2.1 above.
>
> 'Upon service of the Notice, the Republic of Zambia *hereby consents to the award of a judgment* by the High Court in England for the full amount of the Debt together with interest both before and after judgment at a rate of 8 per cent per annum compounding quarterly but after having given credit for any amounts already received pursuant to Clause 2.1 above.'[16]

There are two categories of default clauses:

- non-performance by a party of a particular provision under the agreement;
- occurrence of an event which has been specifically defined as amounting to an event of default.

The Legal Debt Clinic's workshops recommend that a borrowing country should always include natural calamities as an event of default. The borrowing country should be able to enlarge the scope of the events of default.

Usually, the events of default provisions allow a grace period (the minimum is 15 days and the maximum can be three months) after a default occurs to allow the defaulting party to take action to remedy the default. The non-defaulting party can be required to grant the defaulting party more time to remedy the default before the non-defaulting party can terminate the agreement. So, when asking for a grace period, the longer it is, the better.

Before terminating the contract, the non-defaulting party must:

- Declare that the occurrence constitutes an event of default;
- Ask for immediate performance under the contract by the defaulting party;

- Ask for interest for the defaulted period at a higher rate, known as the default interest rate.

It is important to remember that if an event of default occurs, the consequences for the defaulting party will be very serious.

Types of events of default

The following are the most common events of default:

- **Late payment of amounts due**

Failure to pay when the repayment is due is considered an event of default in all loan agreements. This is important where parties to the agreement are highly sensitive about punctual payment. The exact definition of the default event is also important. Does it mean no payment at all or failure to pay the full amount? In the former case, part payment will not amount to a default payment. This shows that it is essential to read the wording of the event of default clause carefully.

- **Breach of obligations**

If a party fails to perform a particular obligation, it can be assumed as a default. However, before considering that this failure gives a right of termination by the non-defaulting party, reasonable time to remedy the fault should be given.

- **Misrepresentation and warranty**

If one party makes a statement, representation or warranty when the loan agreement is signed which in time appears to be false, it enables the other party to treat the change in the circumstances as a default.

- **Cross default**

A cross default is when a default occurs by one party in one particular agreement and the non-defaulting party can construe that there will be a default in another agreement which is not related to the present agreement. The non-defaulting party anticipates that defaults committed in the present agreement will result in the commission of default in other contracts.

- **Material adverse change default**

If there is a material change in the position of a party to a loan agreement, the non-defaulting party can as of right call for a default by the defaulting party. It is safer for the borrower to include a comprehensive set of covenants and warranties in the agreement, where the special circumstances creating the material adverse change are well-defined.

> **An example from the AfDB loan agreement**
>
> Cross-suspension (instead of the term cross default)
>
> - The Fund, the Bank or any Bank Managed Fund has suspended in whole or in part the right of the Borrower or the Guarantor to request for and receive disbursements under any agreement with the Bank, the Fund or any Bank Managed Fund because of a failure by the Borrower or the Guarantor to perform any of its obligations under such agreement or any guarantee agreement with the Bank, the Fund or the said Bank Managed Fund.

Conclusion

This chapter explains what a loan agreement is and has outlined the main types of agreement. It describes its basic structure and gives an overview of the concepts and clauses in a loan agreement that are relevant to the way vulture funds operate. These concepts will appear again in the discussion of cases and examples in later chapters.

The chapter provides several lessons for borrowers about ways to avoid lawsuits. These are lessons which have emerged from the experiences of the Legal Debt Clinic.

To recap the main tips:

- A loan agreement is a legally binding document between the borrower and the lender entailing respective obligations to be fulfilled by each party.

- As regards standard terms and conditions in a loan agreement, it is always worth reading them through and challenging their validity, especially when there is a volatile financial market, even though they appear to be non-negotiable.

- For conditions precedent, it is always advisable to obtain a legal opinion before signing an agreement. Once the conditions precedent are fulfilled, legal implications will follow.

- As regards default, it is important to remember that if an event of default occurs, the consequences for the defaulting party will be very serious. When asking for a grace period, the longer the better.

- Inserting clauses such as CACs protects a borrower's interest.

- Knowledge and understanding of the clauses and terms outlined in this chapter are helpful when negotiating a loan agreement.

- The terms and conditions of a loan agreement can have detrimental effects.

Further reading

- AfDB, 'General Conditions Applicable to the African Development Bank Loan Agreements and Guarantee Agreements (Sovereign Entities)', http://www.afdb.org/fileadmin/uploads/afdb/Documents/Legal-Documents/30774810-EN-NEW-GENERAL-CONDITIONS-ADB-SOVEREIGN.PDF, accessed on 12 March 2010.

CHAPTER 3
Lawsuits

A law is something which must have a moral basis, so that there is an inner compelling force for every citizen to obey.

Chaim Weizmann (1874–1952)

In an ideal world resolving the huge indebtedness of the HIPC countries by forgiving their outstanding debt would be the best option for avoiding litigation. But in the real world, especially with vulture fund creditors buying up sovereign distressed debt, recourse to lawsuits is the only method through which creditors can recover their money. This chapter will trace the historical evolution of vulture fund lawsuits and the legal principles on which they are based.

When the IFIs and the wealthy nations called on creditors to participate voluntarily in debt relief initiatives, not enough thought was given to the various categories of creditors operating in the borrowing and lending market. The IFIs had no difficulty forgiving or restructuring past debts, but there were many reluctant bilateral and commercial creditors who were not willing to participate in debt relief initiatives. At the same time, the market was full of potential investors who wanted to benefit from a situation where there were disappointed creditors. Failure to participate in the debt relief initiatives did not alter any of the legal rights of the creditors, or the obligations of the sovereign debtor under an existing loan agreement. Nor could the initiatives compel a dissatisfied creditor to continue to do business with a sovereign debtor which was failing in its obligations. The possibility of obtaining a return for the defaulted debt on the secondary market remained a strong option for the reluctant creditor, albeit at a much lower return than that owed by the sovereign debtor.

A secondary creditor has no alternative but to lodge a proceeding in court in order to obtain a windfall return on its investment. Lawsuits lodged by vulture funds against sovereign debtors are simply exploitation of an investment space created by the debt relief mechanisms. It has been observed that most vulture funds have been established specifically with the aim of buying distressed debts.

The tactics adopted by vulture funds during lawsuits have disempowered sovereign debtors and pose a serious threat to their ability to restructure their debt or to tackle unsustainable debt. The lawsuits have affected countries in their relationships with their business partners both on a national and international level. Countries' reputations in the international market have been tarnished. Some investors have refrained from proceeding with potential investments. Others who have already invested have themselves been targeted by vulture funds. All in all, lawsuits have increased the risk for investors. Vulture funds not only litigate against debtor countries. They also pursue claims against solvent companies who are doing business in the HIPC countries, with the sole aim of recovering their money.

This chapter illustrates the historical evolution and legal principles which form the basis of vulture fund lawsuits by looking at reported decisions. Most of the cases analysed have taken place in the London and New York courts. They highlight some of the legal principles involved and the effects they have on the economies of sovereign states.

The cases outlined in this chapter highlight:

- Legal defences that can be raised by the sovereign debtor, such as sovereign immunity, the doctrine of international comity, and champerty and maintenance principles. Court appearances and appeals are also discussed (Section 3.1);

- Legal arguments supporting vulture fund claims in court, such as *pari passu* clauses, assignment clauses and garnishee orders (Section 3.2);

- The effects of lawsuits on sovereign states and how they have affected the HIPC countries in restructuring their debts by diverting resources freed under debt relief, blocking money intended for economic development and even holding the state hostage (Section 3.3).

3.1 Legal defences available to a sovereign debtor

Sovereign immunity

The question of state immunity often arises in the workshops held by the Legal Debt Clinic. How can this legal principle help countries avoid falling into the clutches of vulture funds? How can attachment orders against the property of sovereign states which are considered immune from any suit or attachment be avoided?

This section explains the doctrine of absolute and restrictive immunity.

It explains two types of sovereign immunity arising from this doctrine:

- immunity from jurisdiction;

- immunity from enforcement.

It then explains waiver of immunity. Finally, it discusses cases which illustrate why sovereign states have been subject to lawsuits.

Absolute and restrictive immunity

What is state immunity? The saying 'The king (or queen) can do no wrong' has been incorporated into modern law through the doctrine of absolute state immunity. Based on the principle of sovereignty, traditionally state immunity was considered absolute. The sovereign is immune from civil or criminal prosecution as the state cannot commit any legal wrong. It also means that the state cannot be subjected to the jurisdiction and exercise of power of the courts of another sovereign without its consent. However, this absolute rule has been increasingly perceived as an anomaly. As government participation in business matters grew, the rule gave states and state-owned entities an unfair advantage over private sector entities. A distinction was then drawn between public and private state activities. They were labelled in Latin as: *acta jure imperii* (acts of government) and *acta jure gestionis* (acts of a commercial nature). This distinction brought in the doctrine of restrictive immunity.

Immunity from jurisdiction

Immunity from jurisdiction means that a state cannot be tried by a foreign state. Such immunity from jurisdiction is granted only for acts of government and not for commercial acts. In the 1970s, several countries passed legislation regarding the restrictive doctrine of state immunity.

In the UK, the law providing for state immunity is the UK State Immunity Act 1978.[17] In the USA, the relevant law is the US Foreign Sovereign Immunity Act 1976 (FSIA)[18]. Both laws cover the rule and the exceptions of invoking sovereign immunity, and when it can be waived or does not apply. In both UK and US law, the legislation does not provide for immunity from civil suit for any commercial transaction undertaken by the sovereign. These principles, giving rise to the restrictive doctrine of state immunity, have been applied worldwide except in China.

When two states enter into a commercial contract, immunity from legal action will usually be provided for in the contract. If the borrowing sovereign state defaults and the contract is bought by a vulture fund, the country is advised to verify the provisions regarding immunity from lawsuit in the settlement agreement.

In the case of Zambia, there was provision for mutual sovereign immunity between Zambia and Romania. When Donegal International Ltd purchased Zambia's debt from Romania, it made Zambia sign a settlement agreement which waived state immunity. Had Zambia refused to sign the agreement, or negotiated it properly, it would still have had immunity in Donegal's lawsuit, as the debt was assigned from Romania to Donegal subject to equities. In other words, the new assignee, Donegal, would have had to accept all the terms and conditions stated for Romania.

As a rule nowadays, immunity from jurisdiction may not be invoked between commercial creditors, especially if the subject matter of the contract is in the nature of a commercial activity. It is important to note the definition of commercial activity, as it contributes to an understanding of whether immunity from jurisdiction may or may not be invoked during litigation.

A definition provided under US law which is commonly utilised in most cases is:

- A 'commercial activity' means either a regular course of commercial conduct or a particular commercial transaction or act. The commercial character of an activity shall be determined by reference to the nature of the course of conduct or particular transaction or act, rather than by reference to its purpose.
- A 'commercial activity carried on in the USA by a foreign state' means commercial activity carried on by such state and having substantial contact with the USA.

Immunity from enforcement

The second type of immunity relates to immunity from enforcement measures.

In UK law, Section 13 (2) and (4) of the UK State Immunity Act 1978 is important. This states that the property of a state shall not be subject to any process for the enforcement of a judgment or arbitration award or in an action *in rem* for its arrest, detention or sale. But this paragraph does not prevent the issue of any process in respect of a property which is intended to be used for commercial purposes.

Similarly, under US law, enforcement measures will only apply if the property is or was used for the commercial activity upon which the claim is based.

Enforcement measures against the property of a state may have drastic effects on a state. The conditions for the denial or grant of immunity from enforcement measures are still controversial.

A judgment creditor may find it very difficult to enforce its judgment against a sovereign state, as courts appear to be sensitive about indebted countries. In addition, enforcing a judgment will be difficult if a state enjoys immunity from jurisdiction. The courts of the state where the enforcement measure is sought are entitled to examine the conditions surrounding immunity from jurisdiction and the purpose of the object of the execution.

Waiver of immunity

Waiver of immunity means that the state agrees to have its immunity from lawsuit lifted if the state defaults in its obligations or if another party defaults on its obligations. In other words, the state can sue and be sued. This waiver appears in most commercial contracts and especially in loan agreements. Creditors can expressly impose such a condition on the sovereign debtor. Once the state waives its immunity it can be sued before the jurisdiction under the applicable law provided in the contract. In addition, consent to waive immunity cannot be withdrawn after it is made.

In most cases, the Legal Debt Clinic has encountered, countries have wrongly agreed to settle out of court, without even examining the sovereign immunity defence. In the case of Zambia, it was clear that Zambia could have argued sovereign immunity, as the original contract was with another sovereign state.

It is important to highlight one jurisdiction which adheres to the doctrine of absolute state immunity even when involved in commercial transactions. In 2007, in *FG Hemisphere Associates, LLC v DR Congo & China Railway Groups and Ors*,[19] the judge noted that the People's Republic of China adheres to the doctrine of absolute immunity, whereas most countries have opted for restrictive immunity.

In addition, it is essential to note that central banks always enjoy immunity from enforcement measures.

Why sovereign states have been subject to lawsuits

The principle of sovereign immunity, as explained above, gives sovereign states an unfair advantage over private entities. When sovereign states started to engage in international commercial transactions, the issue of sovereign immunity had to be revised. Agreeing to waive their immunity from lawsuit was the first trade-off by sovereign states that made them vulnerable to suits from their creditors if they defaulted.

Two cases illustrate the issues surrounding loss of sovereign immunity. In the first, involving Costa Rica, the court had to interpret a clause to examine whether sovereign immunity was expressly waived.

Libra Bank Ltd v Banco Nacional de Costa Rica 1981[20]

In 1981, Costa Rica was sued for the first time in the US courts when the Bank of Costa Rica defaulted on its debt repayments. This was also the first occasion on which a creditor bank brought a legal case against a sovereign debtor. The issue to be considered was whether Banco Nacional had explicitly waived its sovereign immunity in the contract with regard to pre-judgment attachment.

Facts of the case

A group of 16 banks had made a loan of US$40 million to the defendant, the Banco Nacional de Costa Rica, which defaulted on its payment. The defendant had a property in New York State and the lending bank moved the court to grant a pre-judgment attachment order on this property. The defendant argued that it had not explicitly waived its immunity from any pre-judgment attachment.

In the letter of agreement signed between the two banks, there was a paragraph regarding immunity from suit. The terms of the agreement were as follows:

'The Borrower can sue and be sued in its own name and does not have any right of immunity from suit with respect to the Borrower's obligations under this Letter or the Notes.'

In addition, in compliance with the terms of the letter of agreement, for every promissory note which was made in favour of each lending bank by the borrowing bank, the following conditions were provided:

'The Borrower hereby irrevocably and unconditionally waives any right or immunity from legal proceedings including suit judgment and execution on grounds of sovereignty which it or its property may now or hereafter enjoy.'

The court had to adjudicate whether these two terms constituted an 'explicit' waiver.

The Court of Appeal held that the waiver was clear and the intent of the foreign state was neither unequivocal nor ambiguous. Under this interpretation of the statute, Banco Nacional's waiver was clearly explicit.

The court ordered the pre-judgment attachment order against the property found in New York.

In this case, the issue of the act of state doctrine was also considered, in that it was argued that the court of one country must not judge the acts of another. However, this defence also failed in view of the fact that the parties had entered a commercial agreement.

In the second case, involving Argentina, the US Court of Appeal clearly established that issuing bonds was a commercial activity and therefore no sovereign immunity could be claimed in this respect by the sovereign state.

> ### *Republic of Argentina v Weltover*[21]
>
> The plaintiff, the Republic of Argentina, brought this matter before the US courts in order to adjudicate that the defendant could not sue the plaintiff as it enjoyed sovereign immunity.
>
> **Facts of the case**
>
> The plaintiff, in collaboration with its central bank, issued bonds which formed part of a stabilising plan for Argentina's currency. The bonds provided for repayment in US dollars. When the bonds started to mature, Argentina lacked sufficient foreign exchange to repay. Argentina unilaterally extended the time for payment and offered the defendant bondholders substitute instruments with a view to rescheduling the debts.
>
> The defendant bondholders (two Panamanian corporations and a Swiss bank) refused to accept the rescheduling and insisted on repayment in New York in US dollars. Upon refusal by Argentina, the defendants sued Argentina for breach of contract.
>
> In its defence, Argentina sought to argue that the New York court did not have jurisdiction. The Court of Appeal held that under Section 1602 of the Foreign Sovereign Immunities Act 1976, the US courts had jurisdiction over the actions of foreign states when they are in connection with a commercial activity which has a direct impact on the USA.
>
> In *Republic of Argentina v Weltover*, both conditions were fulfilled: the bond issue was a commercial activity and the bonds were to be repaid in US dollars. On both counts, the sovereign's immunity from suit could be lifted. Argentina was hence sued before the court.

International comity defence

International comity is a judicial doctrine that allows the recognition by one nation within its territory of another nation's legislative, executive or judicial acts. As defined by the Supreme Court in the 1895 case *Hilton v Guyot*,[22] the doctrine allows one country to recognise another's laws. It refers to the notion that domestic courts should not act in a way that infringes upon the laws of another nation. This treatment is afforded as long as they are consistent with US law and policy.

In the case of *Pravin Banker Associates Ltd v Banco Popular del Peru and the Republic of Peru*,[23] Banco Popular asked for a delay to allow for the restructuring of the debt in its country (Peru). The US court granted an initial period of six months. However, granting a longer period was construed by the judge as being against the comity defence principle in the USA, especially when extending the comity would be contrary to the policies or prejudicial to the interests of the USA between commercial creditors.[24]

It should be pointed out that this defence is not a rule of law, but a rule of convenience intended to foster good relations among states.

Maintenance and champerty

These two principles may be regarded as archaic, but they are of interest in many countries. Queries about them have come up at Legal Debt Clinic seminars and it has been asked whether they can still be validly invoked in court. Note that the doctrine of champerty differs in UK and US law. The principles were invoked as recently as 1996 in the UK courts in the case of *Camdex International Ltd v Bank of Zambia*.[25]

The principle of maintenance applies if someone provides financial support for litigation when they have no legitimate interest in the claim. Unfortunately, this does not seem to happen in today's financial markets.

The law of champerty deals with an aggravated form of maintenance, i.e. maintenance and a right to obtain a share of the proceeds of a lawsuit. This definition applies in the UK and aims to stop solicitors 'trafficking' in litigation. However, under New York law the principle aims to stop creditors bringing their new claim to court if they purchased the claim with the sole aim and express intention of pursuing a legal action. In order to invoke a successful champerty defence, the vulture fund must be shown to have had an intent to obtain title for the purpose of commencing a court action.

UK courts had the opportunity to pronounce on the defence of champerty in the case of *Camdex International Ltd v Bank of Zambia*. The Bank of Zambia alleged that the assignment infringed the rules against champerty.

The next example is from the US courts. In the case of *Elliott Associates, LP v Banco de la Nacion and The Republic of Peru*,[26] the New York court concluded that in order to succeed on champerty principles in a claim, it must be shown that the buyer of the loan intended to obtain the title for the sole purpose of commencing an action in court to obtain payment. The court held that Elliott did not acquire the debt in order to bring a suit against Peru. But when the latter refused to pay Elliott, the lawsuit became merely incidental and contingent to the refusal. Hence, the court main-

> **Camdex International Ltd v Bank of Zambia**
>
> **Facts of the case**
>
> In 1982, the Central Bank of Kuwait deposited KD15 million with the Bank of Zambia. The deposit was renewed on several occasions and a restructuring agreement was executed in 1988. In 1995, the Central Bank of Kuwait recognised that the Bank of Zambia would not repay the deposit. The Central Bank of Kuwait assigned the benefit of the deposit to Camdex International. The latter notified the Bank of Zambia of the assignment by sending it the notice of assignment and started proceedings in UK courts.
>
> The Bank of Zambia argued that the assignment to Camdex was against champerty rules. The court dismissed this defence as the assignment was made under valid rules and the original creditor was entitled to sell his property to any person it considered fit. In spite of the fact that the Central Bank of Kuwait was to receive a portion of the proceeds obtained from the litigation by way of deferred purchase price, the deal was not champertous.

tained that Elliott did not infringe the champerty rules. The court held that:

> ... while courts have recognized that Section 489 of New York Judiciary Law is a statutory codification of the ancient doctrine of champerty – that is, maintaining a suit in return for a financial interest in the outcome – the Second Circuit stated that New York courts have interpreted the statute as proscribing something narrower than the definition would suggest. The Second Circuit examined prior case law and found that it confirmed that the mischief Section 489 was intended to remedy did not include the acquisition of debt with the motive of collecting it, even if litigation might be a necessary step in the collection process. Rather, Section 489 was intended for the narrow purpose of preventing attorneys from buying debts as an expedient means to obtain costs for bringing suit.

Since the Elliott case, it has been repeatedly stated that the object of the statutory provision against champerty is the prevention of oppression by unnecessary litigation. Such litigation would follow from the right of an attorney to purchase a claim for the sole purpose of enforcing it in the courts and obtaining costs from the litigation.

However, it is interesting to consider the following statement made in the case of *Donegal International Ltd v Republic of Zambia & Anor.*[27] Quoting from paragraph 76 of the judgment, Michael Sheehan of Donegal International Ltd stated:

> ... our experience and that of others in this business is that you always eventually

recover. You have a legal claim. Eventually if you litigate and work hard enough, you will always recover a sufficient amount to cover your costs.

It can be argued that on this evidence, Donegal International Ltd's actions should have fallen under the doctrine of champerty. Could it be said that Donegal purchased the debt in the knowledge that litigation would almost certainly be necessary to obtain repayment? It negotiated and paid a minimum price to the original creditor with a view to obtaining the maximum amount owed with interest. It is advisable to explore this principle in any future lawsuit with further analysis so as to extend its application.

Putting a defence and appeal

The Legal Debt Clinic emphasises the importance of simply putting a defence in court and challenging any default judgment by way of appeal. These two actions are in themselves a good defence for a sovereign fund. A sovereign state that defends its case can prevent future surprises and has control over the outcome of the case. It could well be that the vulture fund's arguments are wrong. In the case of *Barbados Trust Co Ltd v Bank of Zambia*[28] (see below), Zambia successfully defended the claim in its entirety. In the case of Donegal International Ltd, Zambia did not pay US$48m – it paid instead only US$15.5m.

In addition, when an appeal is made against a decision, valid defences may be successfully raised. Many orders are not granted by the court when the sovereign defends on appeal, providing further reasons why a vulture fund should not win its claim. Several garnishee orders have been set aside on appeal. In many claims, injunction orders have not been granted or have been cancelled. Sovereigns have also successfully raised arguments using immunity defences on appeal.

Often countries that have put up a defence have benefited in several ways. Some countries that the Legal Debt Clinic has worked with have quickly entered into out of court agreements to settle the debt on the mere threat of being taken to court and have later recognised that they should not have done so.

3.2 Legal arguments supporting vulture fund claims

The *pari passu* argument

The definition of the *pari passu* clause made by a Belgian court in the case of *Elliott Associates, LP*[29] gave vulture fund operations an edge – a reason to opt out of debt restructurings and obtain windfall gains. The case succeeded because the court departed from the traditional meaning of the term *pari passu*.

This section looks first at the original case of *Elliott Associates v Republic of Peru*.

It then analyses the subsequent case lodged before the Belgian court to explain the new definition of the *pari passu* concept.

Elliott Associates had recourse to the US courts to obtain repayment of a loan when Peru called for a debt restructuring process and all other creditors were willing to participate. The case brought by Elliott Associates against Peru was a valid case under the principles of the contract.

Elliott Associates, LP v Banco de la Nacion and The Republic of Peru[30]

Facts of the case

Elliott Associates is a prominent investment fund with its offices in New York City. It was founded in 1977 by Paul Singer, who was its sole general partner (see Chapter 1). In 1996, it purchased the working capital of Nacion Banco Popular del Peru, a bankrupt Peruvian bank, for US$11.4m which was guaranteed by the Government of Peru. The real value of the debt was approximately US$20.7 million. The letter of agreement acknowledging the sale was governed by New York law.

Peru restructured its debt from January to June 1996. Peru's Brady Plan for restructuring was agreed by 180 commercial lenders and suppliers (see Chapter 1 for more on Brady Plans). Under an exchange agreement, Peruvian commercial debt would have been exchanged for Brady bonds and cash. Elliott Associates wrote to the defendants, seeking *pro rata* payment of the debt. The defendants refused to pay, arguing that Elliott Associates was not a proper holder of the debt.

On 18 October 1996, ten days before the exchange agreement was scheduled to be executed, Elliott Associates filed a lawsuit against Peru in the New York court seeking an order of pre-judgment attachment. Elliott filed a case in the District Court of New York in order to ask for repayment of the debt.[31] The debtors tried to argue the maintenance and champerty doctrine in their defence (the rules of champerty are explained above). However, on appeal the appellate court concluded that in purchasing the Peruvian debt, Elliott Associates' primary goal was to be paid in full: the intent of Elliott Associates to bring suit against the debtors was only 'incidental and contingent' to the primary goal.

The court also concluded that Banco de la Nacion had breached the Letter Agreements by failing to pay Elliott the amounts due and owing, and that Peru had breached the guarantee by not paying Elliott the amounts due and owing under the Letter Agreements following Nacion's default. The court awarded a judgment of US$55.7m in favour of Elliott Associates.

Elliott Associates successfully argued the *pari passu* clause (see Chapter 2), which was included in the debt agreement. This clause requires a debtor to treat its creditors equally when repaying its debts. In order to avoid defaulting on its restructuring process, Peru chose to settle the case by paying US$56.3m to Elliott Associates.

After obtaining judgment, Peru wanted to pay the creditors who had agreed to restructure its debt before it paid Elliott Associates. Elliott Associates sought an injunction to prevent Peru from paying the other creditors first. The repayment plan under the Brady Plan was to be conducted by Euroclear, the Belgian clearing bank. Elliott Associates brought *ex parte* proceedings in the Belgian court.[32] The court granted it an injunction restraining Euroclear from proceeding with the debt repayment. Since the deadline for the repayment was imminent, Peru settled with Elliott Associates for the full amount of the judgment and post-judgment interest, totalling US$56.3m.

The argument used by Elliott Associates in the Belgian court regarding the *pari passu* clause is explained below.

> ### *Elliott Associates v Republic of Peru, 12 F. Supp. 2d 328* (S.D.N.Y. 1998)
>
> Elliott Associates argued that the *pari passu* principle allowed it to obtain payment equally and rateably with the other creditors, and that Peru could not pay the other creditors first, ahead of Elliott Associates. The Brussels court agreed with Elliott Associates.
>
> The court held that under the *pari passu* principle the debt should be 'diminished equally towards all creditors in proportion to their claim.' Therefore no creditor could be excluded from the payment.

This judgment was a departure from the traditional understanding of the *pari passu* clause. Traditionally, under the *pari passu* clause all creditors were to be treated equally in repayment terms only in the event of bankruptcy or insolvency. The Belgian judgment enlarged its scope to include *pari passu* not just in the context of bankruptcy or insolvency but whenever a payment is made to all other outstanding creditors.

This interpretation mainly benefited the vulture fund creditors, as bankers do not opt to hold out during debt restructurings.

However, the UK courts have not adopted the interpretation[33] made by the Belgian courts. They have strong reservations about departing from the traditional meaning of the *pari passu* clause. In a vulture fund lawsuit, the sovereign debtor will gain if the UK approach is utilised.

No definite conclusion has been reached about which interpretation to adopt. It can be argued that the traditional approach is likely to be favoured in order to protect sovereign debtors from exploitation by vulture funds. It is now well established that vulture funds' operations are merely an exploitation of circumstances beyond the control of the sovereign debtor.

The garnishee orders argument

Trade within the HIPC countries is severely disrupted by vulture fund lawsuits. HIPC countries targeted by vulture funds are considered as high risk countries by investors. This is because vulture funds not only litigate against debtor countries, but have also started to pursue solvent companies who do business with these governments under the principle of garnishing. Garnishment is a *quasi in rem* proceeding (similar to a legal action brought in court) used by a creditor to reach the property of the debtor that is in the possession of a third party, known as the garnishee.

Under a garnishing order issued by the court, a creditor is allowed to take the property of a debtor even when the property is in the hands of a third party other than the debtor, for instance someone who owes the debtor money. A lawsuit is filed by the vulture fund creditor against the sovereign debtor as the 'defendant' and the property holder as 'garnishee'. Garnishment is used as a provisional remedy or when it serves to protect the creditor's interest. Under a garnishing order the property is not transferred to the creditor until the creditor wins the lawsuit. The creditor can also ask for pre-judgment garnishment if the creditor can show that the debtor is likely to lose or dispose of the property before the case is resolved in court.

The case of FG Hemisphere (see box below) illustrates the power of garnishing orders. If the order is wrongly exercised or interpreted in court, it can have damaging effects on a sovereign debtor.

This case is an example of the extent to which a vulture fund can handicap a country's economy if it decides to opt for lawsuits. There is a real risk for many investors, who can be subjected to garnishee orders through no fault on their part

Once a judgment is obtained, if the sovereign state does not take any action such as undertaking an appeal, the judgment will be implemented. An appeal acts as a stay of execution and gives the sovereign state time to act.

A sovereign immunity claim can be raised by a garnishee as well as by a sovereign state. There is no authority for the proposition that it is the sovereign's exclusive right to raise the issue of sovereign immunity under the Foreign Sovereign Immunity Act.[34]

> ### FG Hemisphere Associates, LLC v DR Congo[35]
>
> This dispute arose out of a loan agreement contracted by DR Congo with the plaintiff, a New York-based investment company. DR Congo defaulted in its payment and the New York court gave judgment in favour of the plaintiff. The plaintiff sought to obtain payment through a garnishing order, since DR Congo had not made any payment.
>
> **Facts of the case**
>
> In 2001, the plaintiff sued CMS Nomeco, an oil and gas company based in Texas. The case was brought by the plaintiff in order to obtain payment of royalty rights for oil from CMS Nomeco and other companies under a garnishing order, as debtors of DR Congo. These companies were making payments in kind to DR Congo. Under the garnishing order, the plaintiff asked for an attachment on the drilling of oil by Nomeco. Both DR Congo and Nomeco argued that the court did not have power to make an execution order on oil which was not located in Texas and enjoyed immunity from legal action, i.e. on property that was not located within the USA.
>
> DR Congo, in the classic manner adopted in all loan agreements, had waived its sovereign immunity. The lower court interpreted this to mean that the waiver extended to any assets, revenues and properties belonging to DR Congo.
>
> On appeal, it was held that the district court had wrongly determined that royalty obligations for oil based in DR Congo constituted property located in the USA as required under the US Foreign Sovereign Immunities Act 1976.
>
> In addition, the appellate court found that the conditions under which exception to immunity from execution would apply were not satisfied. It ruled that the lower court was wrong in determining that the property utilised for a commercial activity in the matter was located in the USA.
>
> A sovereign state only loses its immunity if, firstly, the property is located in the USA and, secondly, is utilised for a commercial activity in the USA. The absence of either of these conditions means that the immunity exception does not apply. The appellate court dismissed the garnishee orders as they were wrongly granted.

Power of assignment clauses

The power of assignment has always existed under law of contract, but litigation against a sovereign state has hardly ever happened. The reason for this is the way in which sovereign states have borrowed. When loans were made by bank syndicates, bankers were interested in maintaining good relations with sovereign states. But when lending expanded to include investment funds, there was no need for the funds to maintain good relations with sovereign states or refrain from seeking redress through the courts.

Assignment clauses pave the way for vulture fund creditors to take over the rights of a previous creditor and aggressively pursue sovereign states for unpaid debts. States have attacked the validity of assignments on many occasions. Assignments have mainly been valid and proper except in the case of *Barbados Trust Co Ltd v Bank of Zambia*.[36]

In loan agreements that date back more than 20 years, an assignment clause was not included. If an assignment clause had been included, the sovereign debtor would have had more control and would at least have been notified when rights were transferred from an original creditor to the vulture fund creditor.

In more recent agreements, assignment clauses have been included. It is advisable to include reference to being notified without delay when an assignment is due to take place. Conditions such as a right of buy-back should be given to the sovereign debtor and must be included before an assignment can be made.

In the case of the case of *Barbados Trust Co Ltd v Bank of Zambia* (see box below) the assignment right was validly questioned and successfully argued. However, there have been many cases where the assignment has been deemed to be in accordance with the terms of the contract. In nearly all circumstances, the original creditor notifies the sovereign debtor of the assignment, but the debtor does not always take the necessary steps. This is mainly because the address for such notification is the office of the High Commissioner of the particular country in the UK, USA or France. The Legal Debt Clinic cautions sovereign debtors about the bureaucratic hurdles involved in sending documents to the appropriate ministry in the particular country. In the experience of the Clinic, some documents have taken more than six months to reach the office concerned and by that time the UK courts have already delivered a judgment.

Assignment rights are usually valid. Countries should act promptly when they receive a notification. However, it is worth analysing the formulation of the assignment clause, as it gives more control to the sovereign to choose the type of secondary owners of the debt in the event of inability to pay, with a view to avoiding damaging lawsuits.

> ***Barbados Trust Co Ltd v Bank of Zambia***[37]
>
> **Facts of the case**
>
> In 1985, the Bank of Zambia took a credit facility through a syndicated letter of credit. Article 12 of the facility agreement allowed any lending bank to assign the debt owed to it to 'any one or more banks or any other financial institutions subject to prior consent of the Borrower (such consent shall be deemed to have been given if no reply is received within 15 days)'.
>
> The plaintiff, Barbados Trust Co Ltd, brought a case against the Bank of Zambia in an attempt to recover the amount due. The Bank of Zambia argued against the validity of the assignment and the right of Barbados Trust to bring the case.
>
> Barbados Trust Co Ltd purchased a participation in the loan from the Bank of America. The latter had acquired its interest from a company known as Masstock. Masstock did not fall within the category of assignee, but both the Bank of Zambia and the facility agent acknowledged that it had a valid title to the debt. The dates of assignment and sale from Masstock to the Bank of America and Barbados Trust Co Ltd are essential to a discussion of the validity of the assignment.
>
> The original sale by Masstock to the Bank of America was agreed in November 1999. Masstock notified the Bank of Zambia of its 'proposed' assignment to the Bank of America on 2 December 1999. The Bank of Zambia did not respond and on 10 December 1999 Masstock completed the assignment in favour of the Bank of America.
>
> The court had to interpret whether the assignment, which was completed before the 15 days' notice, was valid, and whether the Bank of America had a valid title to the debt in the first case.
>
> The court held that the assignment was in breach of Article 12 of the facility agreement. Thus Barbados Trust Co Ltd could not establish title to the debt and its claim failed.

3.3 Effects of lawsuits

A country against which a lawsuit is brought faces serious problems. First, there is the question of whether or not it should put up a defence and how to pay the legal fees. Second, even though a sovereign state can now receive help from the African Legal Support Facility (see Chapter 6, Responding to Lawsuits), it has to bear the unavoidable effects of a lawsuit alone, even after its conclusion. If the country wins the case, this is not a problem. But in cases which are not won by the sovereign state, the enforcement of judgments has brought chaotic results in most HIPC economies. These will be analysed in turn.

Diversion of resources freed under debt relief

In 2007, Donegal International Ltd, a vulture fund very similar in its culture to Elliott Associates, went to court to obtain payment upon default by the sovereign debtor, Zambia. This lawsuit is the most recent example of profiteering vulture fund activities in the UK.

The Republic of Zambia was categorised as a HIPC country and was about to receive debt relief from the international financial institutions. The owner of Donegal International Ltd, Michael Sheehan, analysed the prospect of receiving such funds in part repayment of Zambia's unpaid debt. He wrote to Romania, the original lender, with the aim of buying the distressed debt when the defaulted sovereign, Zambia, was negotiating to buy back the debt.

Letter from Donegal International Ltd to Romania, the primary lender[38]

Michael Sheehan, director of Donegal International Ltd, wrote to Romania in support of his memorandum on the repurchase of commercial debt at 11 per cent of face value and Zambia's Paris Club arrangements reflecting the Naples terms:

We understand that Zambia is not currently servicing its debt to Romania and has not made any serious attempts to reschedule these claims in many years. Furthermore, Zambia is not likely to resume servicing its obligations to Romania in the near term. Zambia's economic situation remains dire, and the country's unsustainable external debt burden makes it one of the countries likely to benefit from the HIPC initiative undertaken jointly by the World Bank, the IMF and the Group of Seven industrial countries. Under the HIPC initiative, Zambia will receive additional debt reduction from its bilateral creditors (both within and outside of the Paris Club). In particular, bilateral creditors may need to write off up to 90% of their Zambian claims and reschedule the remaining 10% over 23 years or more. It is the practice of the Paris club to require African governments to agree a minute to the effect that they will not afford any other sovereign creditor better rescheduling terms than they have afforded the Paris Club. Consequently, we believe that there is very little chance that Romania can expect to obtain more in net present value terms than we are presently offering. The net present value of the receipts from such a rescheduling, which has already been agreed in principle by the Paris Club, would be substantially less than 11% of the original principal amount.

The above letter shows the degree of persuasion used by the vulture fund to convince Romania that it was a better deal to sell the debt rather than wait for Zambia to pay it off on rescheduled terms.

The case was lodged in the UK High Court, Queen's Bench Division, in 2007. The vulture fund obtained US$15.5m for a debt which it had purchased for about $4m. The money was diverted from a country where people were living on less than a dollar a day. The Republic of Zambia, by putting up a legal defence, managed to save US$25m, as the original sum claimed by Donegal International was $40m.

> ### *Donegal International Ltd v Republic of Zambia & Anor*[39]
>
> #### Facts of the case
>
> In April 1979, following a credit agreement between Zambia and Romania, the latter provided Zambia with a credit facility to the amount of US$15m to be used to acquire agricultural equipment. There was no provision regarding any governing law in the agreement. The loan was granted at a fixed 5.5 per cent annual interest on the outstanding credit balance. There was no provision for penalty interest or for any consequences if Zambia defaulted on its payments. In 1982, Zambia entered into an agreement to pay only US$5.5m by instalments over a period of eight years.
>
> In 1985, Zambia was unable to pay the amount due and it agreed to reschedule some of the amounts owed to Romania. Under the Paris Club agreed minutes, as Zambia was committed to repaying all its debts, a debt reduction of 40 per cent was agreed between the two parties (see Chapter 8 for the Paris Club Initiative). The final resolution was signed in 1992. After further discussions, Zambia agreed to buy back its debt in November 1995 from all its commercial creditors.
>
> In April 1998, Romania sent a *note verbale* about the outstanding debt seeking immediate payment. Zambia was given a choice of buying back at 11 per cent of the debt payable within 7 to 14 days or paying 33 per cent of the debt over 23 years with six years' grace or paying back over 33 years with no grace time. Following disagreement between Romania and Zambia about the amount owed, a deadline of 31 January 1999 was set for the final decision. Romania cautioned Zambia that it would have no other option but to sell the debt to commercial debt collectors if no agreement had been reached by that date. But unknown to Zambia, during 1998 Romania had already been approached by Donegal International Ltd regarding the assignment of the unpaid debt by Zambia. Under an agreement dated 19 January 1999, Donegal paid US$3,281,780 for the Zambian debt.
>
> The Zambian Government subsequently acknowledged the validity of Donegal's claim and started to service the repayment. An agreement was reached whereby Zambia agreed to pay Donegal 33 per cent of the principal in 36 monthly

> instalments. This would have amounted to US$14.8m. In April 2003, Donegal and Zambia concluded a settlement agreement about the discharge of the debt.
>
> However, the Attorney General of Zambia noted some discrepancies during the repayment period and advised the government to stop payment. Donegal sued Zambia to obtain payment.
>
> The judge considered many issues regarding elements of bribery by Donegal, but ruled that there was not enough evidence to reach a conclusion on the matter.
>
> The judge also looked into the validity, enforceability and applicability of the settlement agreement and at the issue of whether or not the UK court had jurisdiction. In addition, the judge concluded that Zambia had agreed in writing that it should not be immune with regard to the claim which Donegal would bring.[40]

Judgment was given against Zambia for US$15.5m. There were several reasons for the award of a reduced amount, compared with the original claim. Zambia benefited from defending the matter in court.

The court made repeated references to the questionable practices that vulture funds adopt and lure others into. The case was innovative in this regard and highlighted the moral dimensions of vulture fund activities. The following quotations from the judgment illustrate these criticisms:

'... I regard the evidence of Mr Sheehan ... as so incomplete as to be deliberately misleading, and a deliberate and misleading attempt to distance ...'.[41]

'Mr Sheehan provided no credible explanation for this inconsistency and I am driven to conclude that he was misleading in his evidence at the American hearing.

'... when cross examined before me, Mr Sheehan sought to explain that he had confined his answers at the American hearing ... Mr Sheehan must have realised his responses gave a wholly false impression.'[42]

'I have already indicated that I find Donegal's account of how the Government signed the agreement inherently improbable.'[43]

This lawsuit triggered much debate among politicians, governments and NGOs and established valuable judicial precedents. The judge made strong comments criticising a director of Donegal International Ltd for the first time in a court judgment. These comments brought to light the unscrupulous culture of vulture funds. They exposed the way their methods can frustrate the debt restructuring process in poor countries. But it is clear that even when such actions are viewed as highly immoral, they are nevertheless successful in obtaining court awards.

Blocking money for economic development

This section considers an instance where a vulture fund sought to obtain payment by suing for money which was to be disbursed by a donor country to promote economic development in the poor country.

Belgium planned to provide capital for the development of DR Congo. The vulture fund Kensington International sought to attach the money. The capital was only saved from the demands of the vulture fund creditor by the proactive action of Belgium, which decided to enact legislation to counter such moves.

Belgium's donation to DR Congo stopped by lawsuit

In 2007, Belgium planned to grant DR Congo €10.5m for a thermal power plant and €587,000 for its national television station. Before the aid had been transferred, Kensington International, a vulture fund based in the Cayman Islands, sought to attach the funds in a Belgian court in pursuance of a judgment which had already been delivered in favour of Kensington International in the UK. UK courts heard the case of *Kensington International v Republic of the Congo*.[44] The Belgian Government stopped the transfer and decided to enact a law that prohibited vulture funds from seizing Belgian monies disbursed for economic development (see Chapter 7, Legislation).

The sovereign debtor as hostage

The actions of vulture funds can hold a country hostage until the sovereign debtor surrenders to its demands. The court passes judgment according to legal principles. The recent case against DR Congo, when it was faced with a weekly fine, shows how a sovereign is unable to react once a judgment has been obtained in court.

FG Hemisphere v DR Congo[45]

Facts of the case

In 1980, DR Congo entered into a credit agreement with Energoinvest for the construction of a high voltage electric power transmission facility. The country defaulted on its payment. In 1991, the government acknowledged the debt but made no payments.

In March 2001 Energoinvest filed a motion for arbitration with the International Chamber of Commerce (ICC). Two years later, the ICC Court of Arbitration issued an award in favour of Energoinvest for US$11,725,000 plus 9 per cent interest. The sovereign debtor was also required to pay the costs of arbitration.

Subsequently, Energoinvest filed a case in the USA to have the court judgment confirmed in the USA. The US district court for the District of Columbia confirmed the arbitral award in 2004. Energoinvest then transferred its rights in the arbitration award to recover the claim to FG Hemisphere.

In 2005, when DR Congo failed to pay the amount awarded, FG Hemisphere filed a 'plaintiff's first request for production' application, in which it asked the court to order DR Congo to disclose to the court the following government assets:

- The location of any items worth more than US$10,000;
- Any documents that identified aeroplanes, boats, trucks and cars worth more than US$10,000; and
- Any gold, precious metals, works of art or jewellery.

FG Hemisphere sent the court document by courier to the Government of DR Congo. It arrived eight days after it was filed. Only two days later, the district court ruled in favour of the vulture fund company. The court gave DR Congo 30 days to comply. However, at the time of this judgment the court document was doing the bureaucratic rounds and had not yet been translated from English to French.

To date, DR Congo has not complied with the court's request, arguing that the order is a virtually impossible burden. Nevertheless, in May 2008 FG Hemisphere filed a motion in the US district court for the District of Columbia to hold DR Congo in contempt of court. The court granted the motion in March 2009.

When awarding its ruling, the court held that DR Congo had 30 days to produce the requested documents. Otherwise it would be fined a weekly amount of US$5,000 for non-compliance with the order, to be doubled every four weeks up to a maximum of US$80,000 a week. The fine would continue until the government produced all the documents sought by FG Hemisphere.

The fines are currently mounting and will total more than US$4m in one year. The judgment was delivered on 19 March 2009. (See Annex 1 for the text of the judgment.)

The cases described above are not exhaustive. There are many cases where enforcement procedures or litigation have been very damaging to HIPC countries. Liberia is the most recent. In November 2009, the UK courts granted a judgment of US$20m to the vulture funds Hamsah Investments and Wall Capital Ltd for a debt contracted in 1978. Liberia has suffered from 14 years of civil war and rescheduled its commercial debt to the World Bank in 2009 (see Chapter 8, International Initiatives).

Conclusion

This chapter has outlined key cases and reported the decisions in a number of vulture fund lawsuits. The case law highlights some of the concepts and clauses explained in Chapter 2, Loan Agreements, and how they are dealt with in practice. The lawsuits in this chapter have also highlighted legal principles which:

- No longer support the defence cases put up by sovereign states;
- Have given support to the operations of vulture funds;
- Allow vulture funds to obtain repayment of monies owed.

Such litigation causes further harm to sovereign states. All these cases show the impact that lawsuits can have on a country, and how they can make a mockery of global efforts to eradicate unsustainable debt.

The key lessons that emerge from this chapter are:

- It is essential to exercise great care and take legal advice before committing any agreement to writing.
- An active approach to defending a lawsuit brought by a vulture fund is beneficial in several ways.
- Failure to put up a defence encourages vulture funds in their harassment of sovereign states. Facilities exist that can help a sovereign to meet the legal expenses of a lawsuit (see Chapter 6, Responding to Lawsuits).

- It is important to study case law as an ongoing practice. Such study helps create new angles which the courts can use to analyse cases and may point to new legal defences and approaches in a loan agreement.

- The way in which the governments of Zambia and DR Congo have resisted being held hostage has been remarkable and has worked greatly to their advantage.

- Lawsuits can have a crippling effect on HIPC countries, especially with regard to the aggressive enforcement of judgments by vulture fund creditors.

- Sovereigns should act immediately on court notification or other notices from creditors and should always seek legal advice.

Part II will examine ways in which it may be possible to avoid lawsuits or to mitigate their effects.

Further reading

- Commonwealth Secretariat Legal Debt Clinic, http://www.thecommonwealth.*org/Internal/190714/190927/157583/legal_debt_clinic/*

- Judgments available at http://www.thecommonwealth.org/Internal/190714/190927/157583/180640/judgments/

PART II
Actions and Responses

Lawsuits should always be a last resort and countries should take all possible action to avoid being sued in court. Part I of this report provided the basic facts about vulture funds, loan agreements and lawsuits. Part II considers how countries can avoid lawsuits in the first place and possible ways to respond if court cases do arise.

Vulture fund litigation should not be seen simply as lawsuits. It affects the economic growth and sustainability of sovereign countries which are faced with unsustainable debt. In an ideal world, eradicating the causes that give rise to these lawsuits would be the solution: there would be no more borrowing, no more loans and hence no default on payments. However, we live in a world that is far from ideal. In reality, poverty and scarce resources make borrowing a necessity. Moreover, the unsustainable debt of sovereign states is intrinsically linked to international policies – an issue that will be explored in Part III.

The adoption of preventive measures for tackling lawsuits therefore calls for properly negotiated loan agreements to deal with the necessary evil of borrowing, and proper debt management to reduce negative impacts on economic growth.

Chapter 4, Negotiation, highlights how lawsuits can be avoided through capacity building in negotiating skills among officials in the relevant ministries.

Chapter 5, Debt Management, highlights how adopting prudent public debt management will allow a sovereign debtor to achieve better debt sustainability in the long term and avoid debt defaults ricocheting in lawsuits by vulture funds.

Chapter 6, Responding to Lawsuits, looks at the options available to sovereign debtors if they cannot avoid a lawsuit.

This part of the Handbook, like the briefings in Part I, is based on the experience of the Commonwealth Secretariat Legal Debt Clinic and the lessons learned from its seminars. It also draws on the actions undertaken by the World Bank for the development of sustainable economies, with the overarching aim of helping them achieve the Millennium Development Goals (MDGs). The seminars held by the Legal Debt

Clinic were attended both by legal officials from ministries of justice and by financial officers working in ministries of finance or government departments that deal with sovereign debt. This mixed attendance was an essential component of the deliberations during the seminars and elicited lively exchanges of views, allowing the two different functions to be properly discussed and understood. It shows that legal and financial officials in countries affected by vulture fund activities need to communicate, share an understanding of what each other's work involves and work closely together. For example, a team from a ministry of finance that is contracting a loan agreement should include officials from the ministry of justice and any other ministry involved in the project that requires the loan. Only lawyers will be able to highlight loopholes in the loan agreement and the risks involved in formulating terms and conditions which may become issues in court during a lawsuit. Debt managers should be working in accordance with public debt management as a whole, in order to reduce the country's debt vulnerability.

The aim of these chapters is to outline possible actions and responses to lawsuits which can be adopted by a sovereign state. They analyse different areas which contribute directly or indirectly to lawsuits, taking a holistic approach. They range from briefings and checklists which can be used for training and capacity building to prudent measures advocated by the World Bank. The World Bank approach has been taken up by several training organisations and regional banks such as the African Development Bank, Macroeconomic Financial Management Institute (MEFMI), West African Institute for Financial and Economic Management (WAIFEM), the Commonwealth Secretariat, Pole-Dette and the United Nations Institute for Training and Research (UNITAR).

CHAPTER 4

Negotiation

In business, you don't get what you deserve, you get what you negotiate.[46]
Chester L Karrass, author and negotiation expert

If lawsuits should always be a last resort, what action can countries take to avoid them? Loan negotiation is an essential option at every stage during a loan cycle until all obligations are met and fulfilled. This chapter looks at what is meant by negotiation, and at when and how it can be used to obtain the best possible terms and conditions in a loan agreement with a view to avoiding lawsuits in the long term. It also provides an introduction to negotiation techniques for the purposes of capacity building among government officials in HIPC countries.

4.1 When is negotiation possible?

Clearly, negotiating the best terms and conditions before concluding a loan agreement is a preventive measure that can avoid costly litigation later on. But negotiation is also possible at later stages for different reasons, such as avoiding the effects of litigation. For example, Cameroon settled with several litigating creditors through negotiation, even after lawsuits had already been lodged in court. Negotiation is an option even during the performance of obligations in the event of any difficulties arising. It is usually when countries do not take any action after they have defaulted that the creditor opts for litigation. Even in the case of Zambia, Donegal International Ltd was willing to negotiate the terms of repayment, but Zambia refused.

It is true that in the case of most loans contracted with multilateral and bilateral creditors there is very little scope for negotiation, as the sovereign state is made to sign a 'standard' loan agreement (see Chapter 2). But even in the case of standard loan agreements, the Commonwealth Secretariat Legal Debt Clinic seminars emphasise that the formulation of the terms and conditions must be negotiated. In court, interpretation is essential. Hence, knowledge of the standard issues to be inserted in a loan agreement is important. In addition, negotiating techniques help with commercial creditors, especially now that sovereign states are flooded with different sources of finance. Negotiation with creditors also arises when a default in payment is due to occur for economic or other reasons, or when the country has to negotiate the restructuring or rescheduling of a loan.

It is important to be aware of the scope for negotiation at all stages. While legal officials may be primarily responsible for the legality of terms and conditions in loan agreements, finance officials engaged in public debt management will be involved mainly in negotiating and looking for the best formulation in relation to finance principles. Lawyers make good negotiators, but they are not always involved during the negotiation of a loan. The point at which lawyers are involved in the loan cycle varies from country to country, as the Legal Debt Clinic noted when participants shared their experiences. The failure to involve lawyers is a problem that most sovereign countries are suffering from today.

In addition, the role of lawyers in the phases leading up to the negotiation is vital. Usually in the past, in most indebted countries lawyers did not take part in the final discussions, although now, after much awareness raising, this is changing. This has been very harmful for many indebted countries. The lawyer's role during negotiations and the conclusion of a loan deal is helpful in identifying and avoiding risky clauses which place the sovereign borrower in a disadvantageous position. In addition, it makes the creditor's lawyer careful about its actions.

However, from the very lively debates in the workshops organised by the Legal Debt Clinic over the years, which at times verged on the argumentative, it should be highlighted that both lawyers and financial officers need to work together, be cautious and pay careful attention to financial, policy and legal issues.

On the basis of these experiences, the Legal Debt Clinic realised how important it is to impart knowledge of negotiation techniques to all the officials concerned – in the debt department, finance ministry or legal department. HIPC countries lack such skills and capacity building is necessary. Negotiating techniques are universal and can be applied at all stages. Once acquired, these techniques can be developed over time and in every circumstance.

4.2 What is negotiation?

Negotiation is often defined as a discussion intended to produce an agreement or as a means of resolving disagreements. In the plural, negotiations describe sessions of one or more meetings at which attempts are made to reach an agreement through discussion and compromise. Put simply, negotiation is a process undertaken to resolve a situation of conflict or disagreement in order to achieve one party's main interests.

The disagreement or conflict is not always negative. The factors that give rise to conflict can be complex. In the context of borrowing, it should be noted that the parties involved in negotiation have unequal bargaining power: the borrower has less power and the lender is always in a dominating position.

Negotiating skills, like any other skills, can be acquired with time and experience. Based on repeated requests to the Legal Debt Clinic seminars, this chapter aims to provide an insight into what to do and what not to do during a loan negotiation, offering understanding and skills to equip public officials to meet the challenges of financial negotiations. A properly negotiated contract will always give an edge in court to the sovereign debtor.

It is worth first considering the dynamics of negotiation. The act of negotiating is a means to achieve an end. Negotiation helps a party achieve its interests. The art of negotiation comprises a number of aspects which all lead towards this single goal.

Negotiation is a process of give and take. The act of negotiating is not always an argumentative one. Once the parties have signalled their willingness to talk with each other, it can be a platform for sharing information and reaching a satisfactory agreement. It opens the doors to dialogue to solve any problem that is preventing the parties from agreeing with each other.

Unless there is give and take, negotiations may end in deadlock. So while there is often a situation of subordination and an obvious need for the borrower to submit to the demands of the creditors, there is always an element of give and take. It was often said in the Legal Debt Clinic's seminars that 'the sovereign debtors are in dire need of money, but the creditors are also in dire need of making a return on their investment, and they have to part with their money'.

There is always an element of power bargaining in negotiations, as they involve conflicting interests and risks on both sides. The sovereign countries have to be aware that whilst they need the loan, the creditor also needs to invest its money and will eventually lend. Seeking the best option for the debtor state is therefore very important, while understanding the balance of risks involved. The borrower receives the money immediately, but the lender will only obtain repayment in the future. So there is a greater risk to be borne by the creditor in the event of default than on the part of the borrower. Disagreement arises because on the one hand the risks appear higher for the creditor, while on the other the terms and conditions appear too expensive for the borrower. It is these conflicting circumstances which negotiations must explore, discuss, manage and bring to a workable and acceptable conclusion to the satisfaction of all parties.

In addition, the act of negotiation is subject to other influences, such as the political, economic and social context in which both parties are operating. On a personal level, negotiators may become psychologically and emotionally involved in the discussions, and lose sight of their main goal. Becoming emotional is a normal reaction, but emotional issues must be properly managed, to avoid tempers flaring. Otherwise the parties may walk away from a very good deal or agree to a badly negotiated contract.

Each loan transaction has unique features. As already explained, while loan agreements with multilateral institutions have a basic structure and clauses which cannot be negotiated (the 'standard' agreement), in the case of bilateral and commercial creditors, the terms included in a loan agreement can always be negotiated. Even the settlement agreement with a vulture fund creditor after it has purchased the loan from the original creditor can be negotiated by the sovereign debtor.

4.3 Negotiation methods

A proper negotiation for a loan agreement does not start when the parties finally meet around a table to discuss terms face-to-face. It usually starts earlier at the pre-contractual stage, when decisions are made on whether or not to enter into negotiations with a particular creditor. It must again be emphasised that negotiating techniques can be used at any stage during a loan cycle – pre-contractual, contracting and post-contractual.

This section highlights a set of operational tools and methods that will allow a smooth negotiation, whether around a table, via video conferencing or by any other means. These practical methods are based on the experiences of participants in the Legal Debt Clinic. They are an introduction to the skills needed, presented in the form of checklists which can be used as reminders or as training and preparation for negotiating teams.

Before beginning any negotiation, it is essential to clarify the steps of the process through which a loan is negotiated.

These steps are basic, but essential. Different countries have different processes. Laws and procedures differ from country to country. In some HIPC countries the laws that govern the procedure through which a loan can be contracted are outdated. A recent development has been that only the minister of finance is vested with the power to contract a loan, whereas previously any minister or ambassador was empowered to do so.

Figure 1. Negotiating a loan

STEP 1

Identify loan project and check if it is viable

A request is received for a loan or the implementation of a project. The Finance Department analyses the project's viability.

↓

STEP 2

Get clearance

It is vital to obtain the necessary institutional clearance to proceed. In some countries, approval from Parliament is required before a loan agreement can be signed.

↓

STEP 3

Form team

The negotiating team is set up.

↓

STEP 4

Negotiate

Now the team can negotiate for the best terms and conditions and carry the loan project through to completion.

The negotiating team should include members with different expertise – officers with technical knowledge of the project, debt managers, legal advisers and other senior officials. This team may be the final team that will negotiate the loan agreement or the loan may be negotiated by a smaller unit from this team. All team members need to know and apply negotiating techniques, not just one individual or the legal adviser. They need to apply them at all stages of the loan-contracting process, whenever the opportunity to forward their interests arises.

A robust methodology to ensure effective negotiation involves preparatory work by this team of officers. This involves several stages which many countries overlook. The stages are:

1. Analysis of issues

2. Setting out aims

3. Preparation

4. Planning

5. Negotiation

6. Implementation and review

Before undertaking any negotiation, the team needs to understand what aspects they should be negotiating. As observed by the Legal Debt Clinic, they need to identify areas where research is needed. Time to prepare for the negotiation is often short because creditors do not always give advance notice to the sovereign debtor's office.

Here we highlight some basic issues. This account of the preparation needed by the negotiation team may appear obvious, but it is essential. If followed properly, it will ensure that a safe loan agreement is reached.

This series of simple checklists gives an overview of methods and basic issues. It is based on the Legal Debt Clinic seminars and can be used as an aide memoire or as a training resource.

1. Analysis of issues

- What is the central purpose of the loan project? Has it been analysed and fully explored? (For example, the loan may be for the building of a hospital.)

- What are the secondary issues? (For example, it may be that, given the interest rate at which the loan is being repaid, the country cannot take out another loan.)

- Is the proposed manner of borrowing the best way to meet the need? (For example, has the country first explored the possibility of obtaining a concessional loan or grant?)

- Is the proposed source of funding the best source?

- Have all access to finance options been explored?

- Has the project satisfied debt management committee prerequisites?

- Are there any laws or regulations that need to be dealt with before starting the borrowing process and has this been done? (For example, does the law require any procedure to be met before the contract becomes valid?)

- What are the country's interests?
- Has the level of state indebtedness, revenue and expenses been taken into account?
- Who are the parties to the negotiations?
- What are the interests of the other party or parties?
- What is the common ground among all parties?
- On what basis are the interested parties working together?
- What information is needed from the other party or parties?
- What is the best alternative to a negotiated agreement (BATNA)?

2. Setting out aims

Not all the aims are analysed here. These are just examples of the kind of detail needed in setting out the aims.

- What is the purpose of the negotiations? The aims must be:
  - clearly set out
  - specific (not general)
  - practical
  - realistic in terms of time
- Precisely how much funding is needed?
  - What will be the exact interest rate – agreeing on an exact figure, for instance 2 per cent, instead of less than 8 per cent?
  - What about market rate fluctuations?
  - Have all expenses and revenue, as well as unforeseen circumstances, been taken into account?

3. Preparation

The team members should have a range of skills to ensure effective preparation. This will help them meet the other party with confidence. Most countries fail to prepare effectively, as they are handicapped by lack of information, poor logistics or a badly chosen team. Preparation should cover points such as the following:

- How much time is needed for preparation?

- What information is needed about:
    - the project?
    - the background of the parties involved?
    - the negotiators?
    - facts and assumptions?
- Where can the information be found?
    - from research?
    - from information available on the borrower's side?
    - from the parties themselves?
- What information can be obtained before the negotiation?
- What information has to wait for the face-to-face meeting?
- What are the strengths and weaknesses of the parties involved?
- What are the political or commercial interests of the parties involved?
- Are there any cultural or background differences?
- What type of guarantee will be needed?

4. Planning

Planning how the negotiations themselves will take place is also critical and means thinking through when, where, what, who and how.

- When and where will the negotiations take place?
- What constitutes a friendly setting?
- What is the timetable for the negotiations?
- In what order should the issues be negotiated? Is it better to start with easier or more difficult issues?
- Who will speak on which issue?
- How are tasks on different issues allocated?
- What issues can be conceded?
- What issues must be agreed at the end of the negotiations?

- When will be the right time to walk away – depending on your BATNA?
- How will the negotiations start and finish?
- What is the contingency plan?

5. Negotiation

During a negotiation, it would be wise not to take anything personally. If you leave personalities out of it, you will be able to see opportunities more objectively.

Brian Koslow, US author and entrepreneur

Around the negotiating table, it is important to be aware of the other party's tactics, remembering that they too will have prepared and planned. A successful negotiator will always keep emotional and psychological issues out of the negotiating strategy. This checklist outlines key skills and behaviour to adopt (or avoid) in any negotiation.

Listening and communicating

- Display positive behaviour – agreeing and understanding
- Be polite, diplomatic, respectful and calm
- Be attentive to facial expressions
- Listen attentively and ask questions at the right time

Giving information

- Offer information
- Make propositions
- Build on their points
- Cover one issue at a time

Seeking information

- Ask questions
- Ask for propositions
- Let the other party speak first
- Study counterproposals

Leading

- Restate positions to clarify
- Ask questions to be certain
- Summarise and check
- Create rapport
- Seek clearance

Working as a team

- Discuss with team members before reaching final agreement
- Give due notice before making last minute additions to the contract

Behaviour to avoid

- Negative behaviour – being defensive, unco-operative, argumentative or disagreeable
- Speaking at the same time as the other party or interrupting
- Bullying
- Distracting behaviour such as reading papers or fiddling with documents

6. Implementation and review

Negotiation does not end with the signature of the agreement or contract. Points to keep in mind after signature are:

- The minutes of the negotiation should be signed.
- The responsibility and undertaking of each party to fulfil their part should be well outlined.
- Any conditions precedent should be met, such as finalising the agreement in accordance with the law.
- Follow up the implementation of the contract.
- Check if there are any further conditions to be met.
- Look into issues such as repayments and the right time for rescheduling or buyback of the loan.

Conclusion

This chapter has examined what is meant by negotiation, and when and how it can be used to obtain the best possible terms and conditions in a loan agreement with a view to preventing lawsuits in the long term or to dealing with them when they do arise. It has offered practical guidance about negotiation methods for the purposes of capacity building among members of negotiating teams drawn from different professional backgrounds, both legal and financial.

This is just an introduction to negotiation. When embarking on a loan negotiation, team members may need to seek further training, building on an awareness of what is involved. Such training can be expensive: not many organisations run free seminars. The Legal Debt Clinic conducted its seminars in collaboration with other partner organisations. Two useful organisations which offer such training for a fee are UNITAR and the Crown Agents.

To recap the main messages of this chapter:

- It is important to involve a lawyer from a very early stage in the borrowing process.
- There is an ongoing need for capacity building for both legal and financial officers involved in negotiations.
- Negotiating or renegotiating a sound loan agreement is the most effective way of avoiding lawsuits.
- The negotiating team should include different professionals, with a range of technical, financial and legal expertise, who need to collaborate and share their understandings.
- While there is always power bargaining in a loan negotiation, there is also always an element of give and take.
- Negotiations are subject to other influences, such as the political, economic and social context within which both parties are operating.
- The formulation of clauses and their interpretation is very important and should be matters of concern during a negotiation.
- Understanding the basic concepts of negotiation and using them effectively is to the advantage of the borrower.
- Negotiating techniques can be used at any stage during a loan cycle – pre-contractual, contracting and post-contractual.
- Negotiation does not end when the loan agreement or contract is signed, but continues during the implementation and review stages. This mainly involves issues of debt management; these are covered in the next chapter.

Further reading

- United Nations Institute for Training and Research (UNITAR), http://www.unitar.org/

CHAPTER 5
Debt Management

We recognise that the debt burden constitutes a major obstacle to allocating resources to key socio-economic sectors in developing member countries.

Aso Rock Commonwealth Declaration on Development and Democracy,
Abuja, Nigeria, 2003

The lawsuits faced by HIPC countries highlight the difficulties they face caused by debt. Most debt shocks are also the result of globalisation and developments in international financial policy. Public debt management is a way to make indebted countries less vulnerable to financial crisis and shocks in the international financial market.

This chapter looks at the ways in which a sovereign country interacts with the international market and can implement effective debt management at national level. A sound debt management process is one which follows government policy and operates within the right institutional and regulatory framework. Effective debt management can stop unsustainable debt, and hence lawsuits by vulture funds.

Lawsuits brought by vulture funds are slowing down the progress made by many HIPC countries in obtaining debt relief and achieving the MDGs, in spite of strong support from the international financial institutions. One example is the recent case brought against Liberia in the UK courts,[47] where judgment was given against Liberia in the sum of US$20m to be paid to the vulture fund creditors, Hamsah Investments and Wall Capital Ltd. Liberia recently entered into an agreement with the World Bank to buy back some of its commercial debt at a discounted rate.

Litigation is of course a legal problem, but vulture fund lawsuits are nurtured by the unsustainable debt positions of sovereign countries. The financial, economic and political issues that determine a country's debt position play a crucial role in determining whether a lender will become dissatisfied and have recourse to a vulture fund creditor.

An examination of the historical reasons for the rise of vulture funds (Chapter 1) shows the opportunities for profit arising from indebted countries' failure to repay their loan obligations and their dire need for debt restructuring. Shortcomings in the debt restructuring process have inevitably been exploited by vulture funds through court proceedings against the HIPC countries. It is essential to understand that the manner in which a country manages its debt is important, as it can make it harder for a vulture fund to pry into the country's level of indebtedness. In the case of *Donegal International Ltd v Republic of Zambia & Anor*,[48] Donegal director Michael Sheehan indicated in court that he knew more about some countries' debts than did people within those countries. For example, he knew about Zambia's inability to repay and was able to bargain with Romania.

The Commonwealth Secretariat Legal Debt Clinic, with its brief to investigate vulture fund lawsuits, has looked into the root causes of the problem and adopted a holistic approach to reaching a solution. Its research has concluded that methods of contracting loan agreements in HIPC countries and related laws are out of date. Officers working in public debt management offices do not have the best tools or an understanding of how to implement loan repayments. In addition, economic and political issues play a very important part in a country's ability to repay. The experience of the United Nations Conference on Trade and Development (UNCTAD) and the World Bank, which have participated in debt rescheduling over several decades, have shown the weaknesses of debt management systems in nearly all indebted countries.

Being poor is not a sin, nor is it a sin for a sovereign state. However, managing poverty in a way that best avoids paying for costly litigation is an important option. This chapter aims to give lawyers and others who are not familiar with the topic of public debt management a background understanding. It should enable them to evaluate better the context of the loan agreements on which they are often called to give legal advice.

In a global financial world which is constantly evolving and which can have a serious impact on heavily indebted countries, the need to strengthen and update the functioning of public debt management is very important. For more than a decade, the World Bank has been offering services and products, providing global expertise and supporting countries in strengthening their debt management capacity and institutions. It considers that legal, structural and institutional reforms are needed to strengthen public debt management, particularly in relation to objectives, co-ordination, transparency, accountability and institutional frameworks.

The chapter outlines:

- What sound public debt management is;
- Why it is important in reducing a country's external vulnerability, and the likelihood of its defaulting on payments and ultimately incurring lawsuits;

- Ways of achieving effective debt management; and finally
- How effective debt management can be used to identify loans which may be vulnerable to vulture funds.

5.1 What is public debt management?

Public debt management, according to the World Bank, is 'the process of establishing and executing a strategy for managing the government's debt in order to raise the required amount of funding, achieve its risk and cost objectives and to meet any other sovereign debt management goals the government may have set, such as developing and maintaining an efficient market for government securities'.[49]

Public debt management covers two types of debt: external and domestic. External debt is the amount of borrowing (government and private) whether guaranteed by government or not. It also has two levels – macroeconomic and micro administrative. On the macroeconomic level, debt management is an integral part of a country's overall macroeconomic management. On the micro administrative level, it is part of a broader process of public administration and management. To perform well on these two levels, both the execution of policy and the operational aspect must be effective and form part of a proper framework for public debt management.

Historically risky debt management practices make economies more vulnerable to economic and financial shocks, as in the Asian crisis of 1997. As a result, the creditworthiness of a country is also affected. Countries, especially low-income countries, depend on debt. Excessive reliance on these debts, which are mostly in foreign currencies, bring monetary and exchange rate pressures that are felt when a country is unable to pay or when creditors do not wish to refinance the debt.

When repayment of debt becomes difficult, various long-term and short-term solutions must be adopted. Possible remedies include: lengthening the maturities of borrowings and paying the associated higher debt servicing costs (assuming an upward sloping yield curve); adjusting the amount, maturity and composition of foreign exchange reserves; and reviewing criteria and governance arrangements in respect of contingent liabilities. However, once the creditor is dissatisfied or gives up, and sells the debt on the secondary market, vulture fund creditors step in. Servicing the debt is thus a necessity. To achieve this aim, there should be effective follow-up of payment schedules and checks that there is an adequate budgetary allocation every year.

Who deals with payments and how this is done, and who is responsible for managing this structure will be discussed next.

5.2 Why is public debt management important?

The following quotation from the World Bank explains the need for good public debt management. The World Bank advocates that

> ... *effective public debt management can reduce financial vulnerabilities, contribute to macroeconomic stability, preserve debt sustainability and protect a government's reputation. Volatility of interest rates, exchange rates and debt flows require debt managers to properly assess possible risks and to mitigate them by relying on a diverse range of financing sources, while maintaining borrowing costs at prudent levels. The current financial crisis has made the tasks of debt managers even more complex by increasing financing needs at a time when conditions in financial markets are severely constrained. Moreover, the cost and risk characteristics of many financing options have changed, requiring a re-evaluation of existing debt management strategies.*[50]

Debt management is essential to reduce the risk of financial vulnerability. The experiences of the Asian crisis have shown the extent of the difficulties a hugely indebted country has to face. International bail-out becomes a necessity.

Whilst it is true that most developing countries suffer from changes in the international policy framework and are tied to the conditions imposed by most IFIs, nevertheless a huge external debt does not help an economy achieve sustainable economic growth.

At a time when the world is working together to reduce unsustainable debt in most of the HIPC countries, lawsuits from vulture funds are hindering progress. In the cases of Liberia, Zambia and DR Congo discussed above, money obtained from debt relief has been channelled to repay an outstanding loan after court rulings.

For instance, Liberia has been plagued by commercial debt of US$38m. In 2009, the World Bank agreed to assist Liberia and helped cancel its commercial debt, which was bought back by Liberia at 3 per cent of the total value.[51] Later, in November 2009, the UK courts were approached by the vulture funds Hamsah Investments and Wall Capital Ltd to recognise a default judgment that they had obtained against Liberia in the US courts in 2002. The UK court had no alternative but to make a judgment against the Liberian Government, ordering it to pay US$20m.

With sound debt management (which of course would not have been possible in Liberia as it was in the throes of civil war), this kind of scenario would have been avoided.

5.3 How to achieve effective debt management

Seven basic functions are needed in order to achieve effective debt management policies. They can be grouped into two major categories:

Executive (referred to below as the executive unit), which covers the policing, regulating and resourcing functions;

Operational, which covers the recording, analysing, controlling and operating functions. All these functions are dealt with either by one ministry (the ministry of finance, sometimes with a debt division) or by various ministries, depending on how the country's government is organised.

A strong institutional set-up is essential in order to achieve a meaningful debt management system. This responsibility lies with the executive unit. But many indebted countries have suffered in this respect because of a lack of adequate resources, both financial and human.

In the past decades, many organisations have provided capacity building training and workshops (for example the World Bank, IMF, regional banks, Commonwealth Secretariat, MEFMI, WAIFEM, UNCTAD and Debt Relief International (DRI)). However, it appears that the situation is often too complex and that change requires strong political will.

With ongoing lawsuits targeted against sovereign debtors, the Legal Debt Clinic argues that the executive aspect of debt management is where the fault mainly lies. Lack of robust will could be indirectly responsible for the lawsuits faced by a sovereign debtor. Governments need to set out appropriate rules and new regulations are needed. The operational division only follows, working within the limits set by the executive unit. It suffers from inherent difficulties, even if it has the best possible technical support and capacity building facilities.

The Legal Debt Clinic conducted an assessment of the need to update the laws governing sovereign borrowing in many of the indebted countries. It found that most of the participants identified a need for new or updated laws to support existing legislation.

The executive unit deals with the formulation of policies in terms of its debt strategies in accordance with the government's overall socio-economic objectives. It is the sole responsibility of the executive unit to formulate policies that determine debt strategies and the level of external borrowing, and to plan payments accordingly.

By way of illustration, at the workshop held by the Legal Debt Clinic in Ghana, Uganda's debt officers explained that in spite of several debt strategies to cope with indebtedness in their country over the years, they felt that a cap on borrowing was essential and should be implemented annually.

The executive unit therefore also becomes responsible for the type of laws required so that it can properly fulfil its policing function. The executive unit needs to be independent, well co-ordinated and centralised. It needs a well-defined operational unit, which is usually comprised of high-ranking officials and ministers, the governor of the central bank, economists and government auditors. It also needs effective reporting and data collection systems to provide transparency. The Legal Debt Clinic therefore decided to prepare a framework for fiscal responsibility law that was presented to the Commonwealth Law Ministers Meeting held in Edinburgh, Scotland in July 2008 (see Chapter 9, Ways Forward).

The executive unit is also responsible for proper resourcing of the operational unit. Indebted countries frequently suffer from a huge turnover of staff in their debt divisions because staff are not properly paid and can easily obtain better paid jobs in the financial services industry. There is a continuing need for most of the international institutions, such as the Commonwealth Secretariat, MEFMI and WAIFEM, to continue capacity building in debt management. Governments should investigate this constant staff turnover, which hinders countries in dealing effectively with unsustainable debt. Mistakes are inevitable with high staff turnover and the country suffers.

This chapter does not describe in detail the operational aspect of debt management, except to highlight that it involves different levels of functions. Each level has varying degrees of importance, but strengthens the whole debt management system.

The two most important operational levels which have an impact on the number of lawsuits are the units dealing with the negotiation of the loan and the servicing of debt thereafter.

The unit responsible for servicing the debt works closely with the third level, recording, for which a computerised system is recommended. The Commonwealth Secretariat has developed software, known as the Commonwealth Secretariat Debt Recording Management System (CS-DRMS), which is supplied to most Commonwealth countries, together with ongoing training and support. UNCTAD has also developed similar software since 2000; this has been adopted in 54 countries and is known as the Debt Management Financial Analysis System (DMFAS). Installing specialised software to record government debt has proved to be very helpful in establishing a good environment for debt management.

It is essential to know the key points of the World Bank guidelines that are relevant to avoiding vulture fund lawsuits. Further information is available on the World Bank website.[52]

5.4 Identifying loans which are targets for vulture funds

Effective debt management can offer a means of identifying existing loans that are targets for vulture funds. An effective debt management system will allow a country to:

- Know when it is defaulting on the servicing of its debts;

- Monitor creditors effectively, assess their mood and keep in close contact with them;

- Identify if they are willing to restructure or want to dispose of the debt agreement;

- Know how much money is owed and what steps to take, for example whether to buy out, restructure or reschedule the debt;

- Study those loan agreements and check assignment clauses, law that is applicable to the contract, sovereignty issues, *pari passu* clauses, and other terms and conditions of the contract as identified in Chapter 2, Loan Agreements;

- Identify terms and conditions under the agreement that will enable the country to ask for comparable treatment or similar treatment with other creditors or to obtain relief comparable to the Multilateral Debt Relief Initiative (MDRI) terms;

- Assess the risk, especially in terms of the default clauses and the amount of interest or penalty the country will have to pay;

- Consider at that juncture any other options available to the debtor, including a 'name and shame' campaign (Chapter 6, Responding to Lawsuits).

The following quotation illustrates how this monitoring system will help a country. In the case of *Donegal International Ltd v Republic of Zambia & Anor*,[53] Michael Sheehan of Donegal International stated that he used to have more extensive records of government debts than anybody in the market. Donegal routinely called on ministries of finance around the world and was aware of Romania's debt profile. He was in close contact with officials at the Romanian Ministry of Finance's External Debt Department. He stated: '... if a debt hits the market, we know about it within hours'.

Last but not least, if the above options are not successful, it is imperative to negotiate and even to lobby, using a 'name and shame' campaign.

Conclusion

A poor debt management structure can be a major factor in creating economic crises, as seen during the Asian crisis of 1997. In indebted countries, the government's debt portfolio is usually the largest financial portfolio in the country. It often contains complex financial structures which can generate substantial risk to the government's balance sheet and the country's financial stability. It is only through a prudent debt management system, with sound policies for managing risk, that a government can achieve stable economic status and avoid eventual lawsuits.

This chapter has considered areas where capacity building may be needed in order to strengthen public debt management, particularly in relation to policy decisions and institutional and legal frameworks. Finally, it has pointed to situations where effective debt management and risk management strategies can be used to identify loans which may be vulnerable to vulture funds.

The chapter has again drawn on the experiences of the Commonwealth Secretariat Legal Debt Clinic, which have shown that debt management issues are crucial in dealing with vulture fund lawsuits. The important lessons that emerge from this chapter are:

- Sound debt management practices and structures help governments to minimise risks. Debt management needs to be linked to a clear macroeconomic framework and should be linked to countries' monetary and fiscal policies.

- A fiscal responsibility law can help bring stability to the system.

- There is a need for capacity building in strengthening public debt management infrastructure. The World Bank guidelines clarify areas where reform can reduce a country's vulnerability to international financial shocks.

- There are many organisations that deliver capacity building in strengthening public debt management infrastructure. These programmes should be used until the government decides to introduce measures to stabilise high staff turnover in the sector.

- When it comes to identifying loans that are targets for vulture funds, effective debt and risk management processes are essential to check the profiles of loan agreements and the behaviour of creditors. Software should be used to keep track of all loan repayments.

- Negotiation again comes to the fore and is important for the formulation of clauses in the agreement during the refinancing or renegotiating of loans.

Further reading

- IMF-World Bank Guidelines for Public Debt Management, http://treasury.worldbank.org/bdm/htm/guidelines_publicdebt.html

- Commonwealth Secretariat Debt Management Recording System, http://csdrms.org/

- UNCTAD, Debt Management-DMFAS Programme, http://r0.unctad.org/dmfas/

CHAPTER 6

Responding to Lawsuits

Recognise that the world is hungry for action, not words.

Nelson Mandela, former South African president,
speaking in support of the Make Poverty History campaign

By refusing to participate in the debt restructuring process, vulture fund creditors prefer to opt for court proceedings so as to obtain many times the original amount they paid for the debt. Vulture fund creditors are aggressive litigators, as their only reason for purchasing debts is to make a swift profit. If a sovereign debtor does not want to suffer the effects of a vulture fund lawsuit as described in Chapter 3, Lawsuits, then immediate action is a must.

The HIPC Initiatives require voluntary participation by creditors to write off bad debts. Voluntary participation is a condition outside the control of international financial institutions and they cannot force creditors to participate. In the face of the high costs of defending themselves against litigation and lacking national expertise or resources, many countries have not put up any legal defence. However, courts have had to give judgment by default against sovereign debtors under the terms of loan agreements. (Judgment by default is a judgment given in the absence of the sovereign debtor or defendant from court when the case is heard.) Thus sovereign debtors have not benefited from putting up a defence in court.

On the other hand, from a practical perspective, a rush to court is not always the best solution, even for the creditors. A sovereign debtor which cannot repay is not likely to have many assets which can be seized by creditors. Some creditors know that repayment can be difficult in such circumstances. They nevertheless pursue cases for attachment of the sovereign's assets because of the huge return they may make, even though they may never recover any of the money.

This chapter identifies the legal and other options available to debtors when they are faced with the prospect of litigation. Some measures aim to stop further litigation processes and others constitute international support in technical assistance to minimise the impact of lawsuits. Identifying these options should empower countries to meet the challenges they face when defaulting on payments. The chapter explores the scope for negotiation even at a late stage. It highlights three clauses in loan agreements which have an impact on lawsuits and describes the use of 'name and shame' campaigns against vulture fund creditors. It identifies sources of legal support for sovereign debtors when they are faced with litigation. Like Chapter 4, Negotiation, and Chapter 5, Debt Management, it outlines actions which can be taken, again based on the experiences of the Legal Debt Clinic.

6.1 Negotiation

The Legal Debt Clinic strongly recommends negotiation by sovereign debtors in all its seminars. Its motto has been 'Negotiation, negotiation, negotiation'. Negotiation remains a viable option at every stage. Some countries have been able to renegotiate when creditors were threatening to take them to court, for example Cameroon and Mozambique. These two countries have won positive outcomes and avoided lengthy proceedings through negotiation even after cases have been lodged in court.

Negotiation involves roundtable talks at each of the following stages:

- Prior to litigation
- During court proceedings
- Prior to judgment and post-judgment
- During attachment orders/repayment

See Chapter 4, Negotiation, for more about negotiation and what it involves. Both lawyers and financial officials should be aware of who needs to be involved in any negotiations and their role and expertise. The aim should be to discourage any further steps in litigation.

In addition, in 2008 the IMF stated in its report, *Heavily Indebted Poor Countries (HIPC) Initiative and Multilateral Debt Relief Initiative – Status of Implementation*, that:

> *Active and cooperative negotiation aimed at debt restructuring agreements can be a successful strategy to limit creditor litigation and, where appropriate, should be a HIPC's first line of defense.*[54]

6.2 Contractual terms

Chapter 2, Loan Agreements, examines the main concepts and clauses of a loan agreement, which may have an impact on how vulture funds operate. Here three important clauses that have a particular impact on lawsuits are highlighted.

Collective action clauses

To recap, collective action clauses are clauses that allow the restructuring of a country's debt, as long as the majority of creditors approve. They bind all other creditors and eliminate the basis on which a vulture fund creditor can hold out. A sovereign debtor should always insist on such a clause in a loan agreement, even if the interest to be repaid is higher. However, this clause is only useful in new loan agreements, as such clauses were not used in older agreements. For instance, it is argued that the case of Elliott Associates would not have occurred if there had been a CAC clause that provided for a majority provision to bind all bondholders.

CACs allow a qualified majority of the holders of a bond issue (typically representing 75 per cent of the debt in the case of sovereign debt) to vote to bind all bondholders to a change in the terms of the bond contract. CACs are often used in UK and Luxembourg bonds.

Assignment clauses

It is essential to include a proper assignment clause which defines who the new assigned party can be (see Chapter 3, Lawsuits, for more on assignment clauses). An assignment clause can state that the contract may only be assigned to people who are willing to participate in the HIPC Initiatives or that the assignees will be IFIs or creditors of the Paris Club. (See Chapter 8, International Initiatives, for more about the Paris Club.)

An assignment clause can stipulate that the agreement can only be assigned to a creditor who has similar characteristics to the original creditor. For instance, in the loan agreement between Zambia and Romania, it is argued that if there had been such a clause, then Romania could not have assigned its right under the loan agreement to Donegal International Ltd, as the latter is not a sovereign government. As a result, the sovereign immunity principle would still have applied, as Zambia and Romania had granted each other sovereign immunity from legal action.

In the case of *Barbados Trust Co Ltd v Bank of Zambia*,[55] the sovereign debtor was able to challenge the validity of the assignment clause and the title of the new creditor. The claim by the vulture fund creditor was thus defeated.

Applicable law clauses

To recap, applicable law clauses state which legal system will govern the loan agreement if there is disagreement or default. An applicable law clause is essential in providing safeguards from some attacks by vulture funds. Choosing the jurisdiction of a country that has legislated on vulture fund activities and put a cap on the amount that can be recovered is an advisable option.

Since the USA has been active in seeking to implement legislation to regulate vulture fund activities and the UK has already passed the Debt Relief (Developing Countries) Act 2010, it is argued that these jurisdictions are a safe option for sovereign debtors.[56] The cap provided in both these jurisdictions on the amount which creditors can recover through court proceedings will discourage lawsuits in the long run. Lawsuits and opt-out options will no longer be seen as a highly profitable mechanism for creditors. At the same time, sovereign debtors will have a safeguard as they will be aware of the amount they will have to pay.

This discussion of contractual clauses highlights how important it is not only to get the loan contract right in the first place, but also to study its clauses closely if litigation is imminent.

6.3 'Name and shame' campaigns

Once a lawsuit is lodged and a country is sued, it is essential to take all measures to stop the litigation. Activists and NGOs have adopted campaigns described as 'name and shame' campaigns against original creditors upon default of payment by the sovereign debtor. Two examples of these campaigns against creditors (not strictly speaking vulture funds) are described here.

The first is the action against Nestlé, which sued Ethiopia for US$6m after refusing the Ethiopian Government's offer of a settlement worth US$1.5m. Although Nestlé is not strictly a 'vulture fund' creditor, but rather the original creditor, it withdrew its demand and offered to put back into the Ethiopian economy any money it received from the government.

The second successful 'name and shame' campaign was in Guyana. The Guyana Government expropriated the investment of a UK firm (owned by Booker Sugar Estates Ltd) that operated in the Guyanese sugar industry in the 1970s. The government had agreed to a long-term compensation plan and payment by instalments, which were stopped in 1992. The commercial creditor, Booker plc, asked for payment and sought to take the Guyanese Government to arbitration. Big Food Group, Booker plc's parent company, decided to withdraw the case. The matter was heard before the International Centre for Settlement of Investment Disputes (ICSID), which recorded the proceedings as follows:

Outcome of Proceeding:

The Sole Arbitrator issues an order taking note of the discontinuance of the proceeding on October 11, 2003 pursuant to Arbitration Rule 43(1).

Nestlé v Ethiopia

In 2002, the multinational coffee corporation Nestlé sued Ethiopia for the sum of US$6m. Nestlé's claim related to the nationalisation of ELIDCO by the Government of Ethiopia. ELIDCO was a company majority owned by the German Schweisfurth Group, which was subsequently acquired by Nestlé in 1986. In August 1998, ELIDCO was sold by the Ethiopian Government to a local private company for US$8.73m. Nestlé's claim for US$6m compensation was based on the lack of payment after the government sold ELIDCO.

When the case was lodged, the Ethiopian Government offered to settle for US$1.5m, but Nestlé insisted on being paid US$6 million at the 1975 exchange rate.

At the time, Ethiopia was struggling to cope with its worst famine for nearly 20 years, brought about by climate challenges, lack of rain for three consecutive years and a collapse in the price of coffee, the crop that supported a quarter of the country's population.

In December 2002, Nestlé dropped its claim, following a 'name and shame' process described in the following article.[57]

Nestlé, the world's largest coffee company, was forced into a humiliating climbdown yesterday after a wave of public outrage greeted its demand for a US$6m (US£3.7m) payment from the government of famine stricken Ethiopia.

The company promised to invest any money it receives from Ethiopia back in the country after receiving thousands of emails of protest in response to the story in yesterday's Guardian.

At an emergency meeting in its Swiss HQ last night, senior executives were mulling over the public relations damage. The claim represents about an hour's turnover for a company which posted sales of US$59.36bn and pre-tax profits of US$6.15bn last year.

Nestlé – fearing a consumer boycott of its products across Europe – is considering donating some of the money it is demanding to help feed the 11 million Ethiopians who face starvation in coming months.

Campaigners last night repeated their call for the company to abandon its claim entirely. 'I hope that Nestlé reconsiders and realises they don't need the money as much as Ethiopia. I hope they drop the issue altogether', said Sophia Tickell, senior policy analyst at Oxfam.

Nestlé was boycotted for years by protesters over its aggressive sales of baby milk formula to the developing world, where hygiene standards made breast

> *Last night campaigners were keeping up the pressure, although they warned that a boycott of Nestlé products could backfire by hurting poor coffee farmers in Ethiopia.*
>
> *'Boycotting Nestlé products won't help the poor farmers who sell to the company', said Justin Forsyth, head of policy at Oxfam. 'What people should do if they want to help is to write or email Nestlé and ask them to drop the claim.'*
>
> *By late afternoon yesterday, 8,500 people had emailed the company to complain about its treatment of the Ethiopian government, the fastest response Oxfam says it has had to a campaign.*

> ### Booker plc v Co-operative Republic of Guyana (ICSID Case No. ARB/01/9)[58]
>
> In 2003, Guyana defaulted in its debt repayment to the Big Food Group, owner of Iceland supermarkets. Big Food Group was suing to recover a 27-year-old debt for which Guyana had paid £6m, but owed £12m. The creditor was willing to recover its unpaid debt from Guyana through an arbitration hearing. NGO campaigners caused an outcry and the lawsuit was dropped. The 'name and shame' process was successful as the following article describes.
>
> *With the echoes from Nestlé's claim against Ethiopia barely ended, the Big Food Group, owners of the Iceland chain, have backed down having aroused the wrath of debt campaigners by pursuing a claim of more than £12m in compensation against the impoverished state of Guyana.*
>
> *The company has now said that it will not pursue the claim, although people close to the company suggested there was considerable anger at being forced to give way to a basic principle on property rights. ...*
>
> *The debt was incurred during the nationalisation of the sugar industry in 1976. Guyana has paid back around £6m of the original debt, but defaulted on its payment in the late 1980s.*
>
> *Campaigners from the Jubilee Debt Campaign argued that the company should drop the debt altogether, seeking to draw attention to the contradiction where Guyana is granted debt relief on the one hand, only to have a private company receive some of the proceeds.*[59]

The 'name and shame' process has been successful in deterring original big investors from reselling their claims or pursuing their claims in court. However, in spite of the impact of these campaigns, many vulture funds have not been deterred from litigation and have won massive repayment awards.

6.4 Legal support for sovereign debtors

Another option available to a country faced with litigation is to draw on technical assistance in the form of legal support. Some Commonwealth countries which did not have this support have asked for help. In 2006 the Commonwealth Secretariat set up the Legal Debt Clinic. In 2009, the African Development Bank, with backing from international organisations, decided to fund the setting up of the African legal support facility. This is similar to the Commonwealth Secretariat Legal Debt Clinic, but with a bigger budget and the possibility of assisting with legal costs.

The Commonwealth Secretariat Legal Debt Clinic

The experiences of the Legal Debt Clinic (originally known as the HIPC Clinic) and the lessons learned from it provide much of the material on which this Handbook is based.

In the wake of lawsuits against sovereign debtors, most cases were being lodged before the courts of the UK, USA and France. When sovereign debtors received court notices, they had to obtain legal advice from city lawyers in these countries. They could not proceed until they could pay the fees of such law firms, which could amount to several thousand pounds just for advice. One of the countries the Legal Debt Clinic dealt with was quoted a fee of £10,000 simply for evaluating the letters sent by the vulture fund and advising on whether or not to put up a defence in court. The country decided not to appear in court because of the high fees and the court gave a default judgment. The Legal Debt Clinic advised challenging the default judgment through an appeal and the vulture fund subsequently dropped the case. It was clear that sovereign debtors lacked both the resources and the know-how to deal with vulture fund lawsuits.

The Commonwealth Secretariat has taken the lead in providing legal support to distressed countries. It realised that legal advice was needed to make countries aware of the options available to them when vulture funds attempted to exploit the debt restructuring process and the lack of legal capacity within the sovereign debtors, given the huge fees charged by international law firms.

The IMF and World Bank have claimed they cannot provide such support as they are required to operate with neutrality and impartiality in disputes among members or between members and third parties directly or indirectly.[60] The World Bank's principle of neutrality and impartiality is reflected in its *Operational Policy 7.40*. Unlike the IMF or World Bank, the Secretariat is not bound by these principles, as it does not interact with sovereign countries as a party to loan agreements.

The Secretariat therefore established the Legal Debt Clinic in September 2006.[61] Its mandate came from agreements obtained at ministerial meetings of the finance and law ministers of the HIPC countries. Finance ministers gave their approval at a meeting held in Sri Lanka in September 2006, then known as the Commonwealth HIPC Ministerial Forum (CHMF).[62] Law ministers gave their approval at their meeting held in Accra, Ghana in October 2005.[63] The Legal Debt Clinic presented its annual reports to the HIPC finance ministers, and to the law ministers during their triennial meetings.

The focus of the Clinic has been two tiered: first, it advises on the actions that should be taken following a lawsuit; and second, it advises countries on global actions to avoid legal action. It also gives advice on steps that can be adopted to avoid future lawsuits through an examination of the terms and conditions of loan agreements and helps HIPC countries to negotiate such agreements.

The Legal Debt Clinic has achieved the following:

- **Awareness raising**

The Clinic has made officials in ministries of finance and debt divisions aware of the need to work in close collaboration with the Attorney-General's Office regarding the legal implications of the terms and conditions contained in loan agreements. Successful workshops have been held in Jamaica for the Caribbean countries and in Africa for most of the African HIPC countries. The following workshops have taken place:

Commonwealth Seminar on *Debt Negotiation and Renegotiation*, Kingston, Jamaica, November 2006

Commonwealth Seminar on *Debt Negotiation and Renegotiation*, Accra, Ghana, November 2007

Joint Commonwealth and Pole-Dette Seminar on *Debt Negotiation and Renegotiation*, Yaoundé, Cameroon, May 2008

Joint Commonwealth and MEFMI Seminar on *Legal Aspects of Debt Management*, Maputo, Mozambique, August 2008

Joint Commonwealth and MEFMI Seminar on *Negotiation: Techniques and Practical Skills*, Dar es Salaam, Tanzania, June 2009

- **Bilateral assistance**

The Clinic has also assisted HIPC countries facing threats of litigation and actual litigation bilaterally. Through these meetings it has built the capacity of legal and finance officers and provided in-house training. Such bilateral meetings have taken place for Zambia (May 2007), Uganda (August 2007) and Cameroon (August 2007).

- Capacity building

The Clinic has delivered capacity building in loan agreements and public debt management, fiscal responsibility law, and negotiation techniques and skills. It has raised awareness of the need for a strong institutional set-up of the office dealing with debt management to help countries out of severe indebtedness. It has raised awareness of the eventual need for changes in domestic legislation. It has also provided training in practical techniques and negotiation skills.

- Advocating change

The Clinic has advocated changes in legislation both in the domestic laws of sovereign debtors and internationally in jurisdictions where the lawsuits take place.

At national level, it has advised each sovereign debtor to update and align its public debt laws to feature new accountability and transparency principles. It has recommended the adoption of fiscal responsibility laws which would incorporate a national debt strategy based on principles of accountability, reporting and transparency. The workshops have highlighted and presented a fiscal responsibility framework.

Another domestic change advocated by the Clinic is setting up a framework for the negotiation of loan agreements that incorporates similar rules for most countries. However, there is as yet no mandate for the development of this framework.

The Clinic has also advocated changes in legislation in the countries where the lawsuits take place to stop the profiteering activities of vulture fund creditors, especially after many creditors refused to participate in the HIPC Initiative. Vulture fund loan agreements contain clauses that are highly detrimental to the ability of sovereign debtors to defend themselves in court. The obvious solution is to enact legislation that prevents such cases being heard by the courts in the jurisdictions where these lawsuits are usually filed. This has mainly been in relation to UK legislation, as the UK is a Commonwealth member. In 2007, publicity about the Zambian case on the BBC's *Newsnight* programme generated public pressure against the UK Government, as it appeared that the UK jurisdiction was being exploited by vulture fund investors and that UK courts were a favourite jurisdiction for such cases. In spite of lobbying, it was only in May 2009 that Sally Keeble MP tabled a motion in Parliament on this issue. Finally, the UK Parliament passed the Debt Relief (Developing Countries) Act in April 2010 (see Chapter 7, Legislation).

The African Legal Support Facility

The African Legal Support Facility is another source of advisory support similar to the Commonwealth Secretariat Legal Debt Clinic. It was set up in June 2009 and at the time of writing (early 2010) is still in the process of becoming fully functional.

In April 2008, the executive board of the AfDB approved the establishment of this legal support facility. It will come into existence when the agreement creating it is signed by at least ten participating states or international organisations. This requirement has been fulfilled and the text establishing the institutional set-up of the facility's management structures was published in June 2009. It will have a similar role to the Legal Debt Clinic. It has received funding of over £5m from the UK Department for International Development (DFID) and other international organisations.

Unlike the Legal Debt Clinic, the African Legal Support Facility will provide funding to indebted countries to meet the costs of legal expenses incurred in lawsuits.[64] The sovereign debtor will repay the legal expenses on terms that depend on the status of the country.[65] Lawsuits can be very expensive and help with legal costs is bound to reduce the number of default judgments against sovereign debtors.

Conclusion

This chapter has looked at a range of options available to indebted countries that face lawsuits. It has stressed that negotiation is an option at every stage. It has highlighted clauses in loan agreements which can safeguard against future lawsuits – CACs, assignment clauses and applicable law clauses. Another option described here is 'name and shame' campaigns conducted against creditors. Finally, the chapter describes two initiatives which provide legal support for sovereign debtors.

The important message of this chapter is that lawsuits always have a protracted impact and are a block to any economic development.

- Indebted countries should never 'do nothing' when they receive a notice from the court or the creditor's lawyers.
- Indebted countries should always talk to their creditors and keep in touch to know what action they are considering.
- The quicker a lawsuit is resolved the better.
- Both national and international efforts are needed to resolve this situation.
- Legal advice and support should be sought immediately. This will help to reduce the number of default judgments against sovereign debtors and help countries take appropriate action to respond to or avoid lawsuits.

Further reading

- The World Bank Operational Manual, http://web.worldbank.org/WEBSITE/EXTERNAL/PROJECTS/EXTPOLICIES/EXTOPMANUAL/0,,menuPK:64142516~pagePK:64141681~piPK:64141745~theSitePK:502184,00.html

- Commonwealth Secretariat Legal Debt Clinic, http://www.thecommonwealth.org/Internal/190714/190927/157583/legal_debt_clinic/

- African Legal Support Facility, http://www.afdb.org/en/topics-sectors/initiatives-partnerships/african-legal-support-facility/

PART III

Challenges and Solutions

Poverty is an international problem which involves the international financial community, including multilateral and regional organisations and governments around the world. The HIPC Initiative, established in 1996, is a bilateral and multilateral effort to help poor countries achieve economic growth and debt sustainability. Lawsuits by vulture funds are a major obstacle to such debt relief.

Part II highlighted ways in which a sovereign can avoid lawsuits in the first place and respond to them if they arise. However, when the HIPC Initiative was launched, the multilateral organisations did not envisage lawsuits by vulture funds. In view of the lack of predicted progress towards debt relief (the target year being 2015), further action by the global community is necessary.

Part III considers the challenges the international community faces in dealing with the threats posed by vulture fund lawsuits and describes a range of solutions that have been adopted so far.

Chapter 7, Legislation, looks at ways of regulating vulture fund lawsuits through legislation and argues that robust legislation is the best way forward.

Chapter 8, International Initiatives, analyses measures taken by the international community to reduce debt.

Chapter 9, Ways Forward, discusses possible further solutions for reducing the negative effects of lawsuits worldwide. Could an organised structure with codes of borrowing and lending or a single dispute resolution mechanism other than the courts be solutions?

CHAPTER 7

Legislation

We have seen that nothing short of legislation will stop these investors from their outrageous practices.

Nick Dearden, Director of the Jubilee Debt Campaign[66]

Whatever the hopes and whatever moral pressure is applied, there has been increasing recognition that without legislation to regulate vulture funds it will be difficult to stop their exploitative practices.

Jurisdictions such as those of the UK, USA and France have been very involved, since commercial creditors opt for the favourable law of contract of these countries in nearly all loan agreements. Whilst commercial creditors can easily afford to defend cases in these countries, sovereign debtors cannot. The negative outcome of a lawsuit has even more devastating consequences for a country than its immediate socio-economic effects, especially if the lawsuit is not dealt with properly from a legal perspective. It is a mistake to consider this as a purely socio-economic issue which can be dealt with on a voluntary basis or by passing moral judgements.

According to the law of contract, both parties are bound by their intentions and their intentions are reflected in the loan agreement. In such cases it is impossible to ask the court to interpret the obligations of the sovereign debtor in a manner contrary to the stipulations made in the agreement. The only exception that can be validly used to cancel the obligation of either party is if the nature of the contract is against public order. Even if it is clear that aggressive litigation by a vulture fund is disrupting the greater global good, the court still has to interpret according to the terms of the loan agreement. In the recent vulture fund case of Hamsah Investments and Wall Capital Ltd brought against Liberia in the UK courts, the judge, Mr Justice Burton, said:[67]

The only issue raised is plainly a sad one, that Liberia is a poor country, and cannot afford it.

This chapter outlines legislative action taken in a number of countries to regulate unfair practices in an attempt to help indebted countries. It looks at the jurisdictions of Belgium, the UK, the USA and France.

7.1 Belgian law (2008)

Belgium was the first country to make a strong legal commitment to help countries achieve sustainable debt. The Belgian Government has contracted many loans to Congo-Brazzaville and DR Congo. In 2007, ten lawsuits were lodged against DR Congo in Belgian courts. Some of these asked the courts to validate the judgments which vulture funds had obtained in their favour in other foreign courts. Enforcement of judgments is a crucial factor in vulture funds' success in lawsuits.

In January 2008, Belgium set a precedent by passing a legal resolution to 'safeguard Belgian funds disbursed towards development co-operation and debt relief from the actions taken by vulture funds'. The legislation came into operation in April 2008 after being voted on and published in accordance with Belgium's constitutional requirements. The law is very concise and provides that no monies granted by the Belgian authorities can be seized by or transferred to vulture funds or any other creditor. This legislation has automatically barred any vulture fund from pursuing any Belgian money or companies investing in the sovereign debtor country to obtain repayment. The members of Belgium's Federal Parliament approved the law quickly and unanimously. The Bill had a swift passage from the last day of January 2008, when it was introduced in the House of Representatives, and became law on 6 March 2008.[68] The Belgian Government is determined to deter vulture fund creditors, which could not challenge this unanimous decision. (See Annex 2 for the text of the Belgian law.)

The Legal Debt Clinic commends Belgium's action and the other steps it has taken to eradicate immoral lawsuits. It believes Belgium's stand should encourage other countries such as the UK and the USA to fight vulture fund lawsuits.

7.2 UK law (2010)

UK courts are a favourite place for vulture funds to bring lawsuits or seek recognition of foreign judgments made in their favour. There are many reasons for choosing UK courts. UK law is favourable to creditors and is often used in loan agreements as the applicable law.

The UK's commitment to debt relief has been stronger since it chaired the 2005 G8 meeting (see Chapter 8, International Initiatives, for more detail). The actions of vulture funds creditors in siphoning off the resources of UK taxpayers by making huge profits from litigation caused the UK Government to act to resolve the situation. Ian Pearson MP, Economic Secretary to the Treasury, stated:

> *These claims, including those brought in UK Courts, mean that poor countries are forced to pay back some of their outstanding debt in full and with the addition of interest. The nature of these cases means that a small minority of creditors can divert some of the benefits of debt relief provided by the majority. The government is determined that these actions do not prevent poor countries from using the resources freed up by debt relief for development and poverty reduction. And we firmly believe it is right to act to prevent this from happening at the expense of debt relief funded by the UK taxpayer.*[69]

After much campaigning for reform of the legislation, Labour MP Sally Keeble introduced a Bill in May 2009 under the ten-minute rule. This rule allows a Member of Parliament to bring an important issue to the attention of the government, although the Bill may not make it into law. The government decided to launch a consultation paper on vulture funds in July 2009.[70]

The Bill introduced by Sally Keeble was entitled 'Developing Country Debt (Restriction of Recovery) Bill'. It aimed to clip the wings of the vulture funds. After its first reading it received cross-party support and was backed by around 160 MPs.[71] Its main provisions were:

- To outlaw profiteering by putting a cap on the amount that vulture funds can ask in repayment;

- To require more accountability for the secret activities of vulture funds through disclosure to be made to the UK courts before bringing a lawsuit;

- To create transparency, as vulture funds would have to disclose their investors and beneficiaries;

- To ban corrupt payments.

The consultation on the legislation closed in October 2009 and the government gave its response in February 2010.[72] It decided to introduce the Debt Relief (Developing Countries) Bill. Its response to the consultation was presented by Ian Pearson MP, who stated:

> *We need to change the law to prevent creditors from taking this path. Commercial finance can help – not hinder – development in low-income countries. The Private Member's Bill seeks to prevent creditors from recovering an amount in excess of the debt relief expected. The Government, which consulted on legislation last year, will be supporting the Bill when it is debated on 26 February. Parliament has*

a chance to make sure that millions of the world's poorest people gain maximum benefit from the debt relief that we provide. Parliamentarians from across the political spectrum can bring this about by helping the Bill to become law.[73]

In February 2010, the Bill had its second reading in Parliament. It was passed into law at the last parliamentary session before the general election of May 2010. Known as the Debt Relief (Developing Countries) Act 2010,[74] the legislation will have many positive results. (See Annex 3 for the text of the Act.) According to its sponsoring MP, under its provisions Donegal International Ltd would have obtained only US$3.3m in its case against Zambia, instead of the US$15.5 million it received.[75] The first application of this favourable law will be in the Liberian case, where US$20m was awarded to Hamsah Investments and Wall Capital Ltd in November 2009, which will have to be revised in the light of the new Act.

The UK legislation is of great benefit to the HIPC countries which are at present unable to use monies disbursed to them through debt relief for the purposes of economic development. Once the vulture fund creditors are stopped from profiteering, the countries will be able to use the freed-up resources in the sectors where they are most needed, such as health, education and infrastructure.

Though the passing of legislation in the UK has not been as smooth as in Belgium, it is nevertheless very welcome. It highlights the challenges involved in passing such legislation in developed countries. The effect of the UK law will probably compel the vulture funds to lodge their cases in other jurisdictions such as the USA or France. This is so that they can continue to make huge profits from such lawsuits. However, surprisingly, the UK law has an expiry date and is valid only for one year beginning in April 2010. The UK Treasury will then have the power to give the law permanent effect.

Poor countries and campaigners will now have to concentrate their efforts on the USA to ensure that a similar law is passed there; they must also wait and see what the UK Parliament will decide in a year's time.

7.3 US law (2008 and 2009)

In August 2008, a Bill was introduced into the US Congress under H.R. 6796. It was known as the 'Stop Very Unscrupulous Loan Transfers from Underprivileged Countries to Rich, Exploitative Funds Act'.[76] This Bill never made it into law, but was referred to two committees.

In June 2009, Representative Maxine Waters (Democrat, California) reintroduced the US Stop Vulture Funds Bill (H.R. 2932)[77] to outlaw profiteering by vulture funds. This draft law is similar to the UK Debt Relief (Developing Countries) Act.

The Stop Vulture Funds Bill aims to cap the amount of profit which a secondary creditor can reap through litigation based on defaulted sovereign debts. Before any such litigation can be pursued in the US courts, the Bill requires public disclosure of the names of any persons with an interest in the sovereign debt claim, how and where the claim was acquired and the purchase price. The Bill also requires vulture funds to certify that they have not given any bribe while acquiring or pursuing collection of the defaulted debt claim.

The Stop Vulture Funds Bill[78] prohibits:

1. Any US person from engaging in sovereign debt profiteering, or any person from engaging in such profiteering in the USA; and

2. Any US court from issuing a summons, subpoena, writ, judgment, attachment or execution in aid of a claim which would further sovereign debt profiteering. The legislation sets forth required court disclosures in actions involving the collection of sovereign debt.

The proposed legislation is gaining momentum and has been co-sponsored by many other representatives. The legislation now needs the support of the full House and to be moved for Senate review.

7.4 French law (2007)

In August 2007, Marc Le Fur presented a law before the French Assembly to fight the actions of vulture funds.

The proposed law, which has not yet been passed, is based on a principle similar to the champerty rules (explained in Chapter 2, Loan Agreements). The law has two purposes. First, it aims to stop vulture fund creditors using the French courts to validate judgments obtained before foreign courts. Second, it aims to allow vulture fund creditors to claim only the amount they spent on buying the debt, instead of the debt plus interest. The French Assembly has not yet legislated on this.

Conclusion

The legislative initiatives outlined in this chapter show that legislation is seen as essential to regulate the unfair practices of vulture funds, although it is not the only solution. If nothing is done by legislatures and if the matter is left to voluntary action by the vulture funds or to the courts, the efforts of all those countries which have been willing to work together to eradicate poverty and help countries attain the MDGs will be defeated. But there are many challenges in passing legislation. The most recent case against Liberia lodged in London in November 2009, where the UK courts ordered Liberia to pay US$20m to its vulture fund creditors, shows that free riding by vulture funds on debt relief has not as yet been stopped. Instead, debt relief mechanisms are making enforcement of the judgments more feasible, with the vulture funds calculating that the indebted country will eventually have to pay. It will be interesting to note the reaction of the vulture funds when the court revises the amount to be paid in accordance with the UK Debt Relief (Developing Countries) Act 2010.

The key messages of this chapter are:

- The challenges faced in passing legislation show that the applicable law clause in agreements (explained in Chapter 2, Loan Agreements) will be increasingly important in taking advantage of favourable jurisdictions.
- Once again, it is clear that the preferred solution available to sovereign debtors is negotiation of a safer loan agreement or settlement agreement when a new creditor takes over the rights of the original creditor.
- Without further solutions (outlined in Chapter 9, Ways Forward) and legislation to stop profiteering, vulture funds will continue to take action until all unsettled debts sold to them are paid in one way or another.

Further reading

UK Parliament, http://www.parliament.uk/

US House of Representatives, http://www.house.gov/

Debt Relief (Developing Countries) Act 2010, http://www.opsi.gov.uk/acts/acts2010/pdf/ukpga_20100022_en.pdf

Annex 3 of this Handbook, UK Debt Relief (Developing Countries) Act 2010

CHAPTER 8

International Initiatives

So it is to be hoped that ... the process of debt cancellation and reduction for the poorest countries will be continued and accelerated.

Pope Benedict XVI, 8 January 2007

Heads of government, civil society, the IMF and the World Bank have condemned the behaviour of vulture funds. Ongoing lawsuits have highlighted an increasing need for support from the international community. One successful step has been an increase in debt relief, which has ultimately prevented many bilateral creditors from selling their claims to the vulture funds. This has in turn helped to avoid many lawsuits.

This chapter outlines the main debt relief initiatives and what they have achieved in curtailing the crippling debt of poor countries.

8.1 HIPC debt relief initiatives (1996)

In the 1990s, many poor countries faced a debt crisis. Interest payments were costing more than the countries were investing in new infrastructure. The IFIs and regional banks recognised that the debts could not be repaid. In response, in 1996 the IMF and the World Bank introduced the HIPC Initiative as a debt reduction package. The IMF and the World Bank aimed to ensure that poor countries were not encumbered with unmanageable debt. Under the HIPC Initiative, indebted countries were categorised as HIPCs and non-HIPCs. Some 40 countries were initially targeted as HIPCs. These countries received debt write-offs, conditional on their implementing certain measures, namely adjustment and reform programmes. Once the IFIs considered a HIPC country eligible for debt relief, they hoped other commercial or bilateral creditors would join in and write off debts voluntarily. Unfortunately this did not work out as expected, as creditors started to sell their debts on the secondary market.

The HIPC Initiative was reviewed in 1999 to provide for more effective debt relief and to strengthen the links between debt relief, poverty reduction and social policies.[79] Because of several vulture fund lawsuits, the results were still not as expected, and in 2005 the HIPC Initiative was supplemented by the Multilateral Debt Relief Initiative, which allowed for 100 per cent cancellation of debt on eligible debts.

In order to make debt relief more effective, the World Bank Debt Reduction Facility (DRF) made grant funding available to eligible governments to buy back debts owed to external commercial creditors. In the early days of the DRF, grants were given to International Development Association (IDA) indebted countries only to fund buy-back operations. So far, the DRF has been the most effective agency in stopping original creditors from selling their debts to vulture fund creditors. In Nicaragua, the DRF supported buy-backs of debt and four lawsuits were successfully stopped. The DRF also helped buy-back operations in Mozambique and Liberia. Buy-backs under the DRF have stopped many commercial creditors from going to court and are cheaper than litigation. Information about the initiatives and the DRF is available on the World Bank website.[80]

8.2 Norway (1998)

Following the introduction of the HIPC Initiative, in 1998 Norway was the first OECD country to present a comprehensive plan of action on debt relief for developing countries.[81] Norway was also the first OECD country to advocate 100 per cent debt cancellation for heavily indebted poor countries. All the political parties in Norway's National Assembly support its debt relief policy.

To date, Norway has provided relief beyond the terms of the HIPC Initiative (which is 90 per cent of bilateral debt reduction) and has given 100 per cent cancellation debt relief. Relief has been given to Benin, Tanzania, Senegal, Ghana, Côte d'Ivoire, DR Congo, Guinea, Sierra Leone and The Gambia. Another interesting feature of the Norwegian initiative is that debt cancellation is not financed out of the aid budget, but is additional to its official development assistance (ODA).

The Norwegian efforts have helped prevent many unpaid debts being acquired by commercial creditors. This has helped enormously in keeping many lawsuits out of court.

Norwegian policy highlights[82]

Norway is determined to:

- Continue to cancel 100 per cent of the debt of all HIPC countries indebted to Norway, provided they complete HIPC procedures;

- Support an extension of the December 2004 HIPC sunset clause to allow, inter alia, conflict-ridden countries, e.g. Sudan, Liberia and Somalia, to qualify;

- Consistently remind the international community that in order to deliver on the promise of HIPC debt reduction, the huge financing gaps that have been identified (e.g. US$11bn in IDA costs) must be addressed decisively, generously and regularly;

- Help pave the way for the clearance of arrears and speedy HIPC status for severely indebted poor countries emerging from armed conflict and civil strife;

- Grant faster and deeper debt reduction to severely indebted post-conflict countries, preferably 100 per cent debt service reduction once credible peace treaties are signed and representative governments have been formed;

- Pursue the Norwegian proposal for bilateral creditors to undertake multilaterally co-ordinated debt-for-development swaps, i.e. arrangements by which several creditor countries join forces in trading debt forgiveness for increased spending on health and education in non-HIPC debtor countries;

- Negotiate debt-for-development swaps with Pakistan, Vietnam and Ecuador, in co-operation with Canada, the Asian Development Bank and the Inter-American Development Bank, respectively;

- Support debt reduction for middle-income countries with unsustainable debt, as part of the Paris Club's new Evian Approach;

- Support the updating of Paris Club 'cut-off dates' to help make sure that demonstrably unsustainable debts are not excluded from debt negotiations;

- Support South-South (HIPC-to-HIPC) debt reduction efforts, provided a multilateral mechanism is established to achieve this;

- Continue to actively support mechanisms to reduce debt owed to multilateral finance institutions (the World Bank's 5th Dimension Facility) and private creditors (the IDA Debt Reduction Facility) in a cost-effective manner;

- Make sure that Norway's debt relief efforts are carefully tailored so as not to benefit other creditors, but only the indebted countries themselves.

8.3 G8 (2005)

In 2000 the UN Millennium Summit agreed the Millennium Development Goals, a series of targets aimed at reducing poverty and improving people's lives throughout the developing world. There was broad recognition that without debt relief and increases in ODA the MDGs would not be achieved.

In 2005, under growing pressure from various organisations and environmental groups to address poverty in Africa and help countries achieve the MDGs, the G8 summit decided to take action. (The G8 summit is a meeting of the world's seven leading industrialised nations, the UK, Canada, France, Germany, Italy, Japan and the USA, plus Russia.)

In the Gleneagles Communiqué, the G8 agreed to increase aid to Africa. Governments offered debt cancellation of US$40 bn[83] and 100 per cent cancellation for eligible HIPC countries of debts to the IMF, World Bank and the African Development Bank. Each G8 country made specific aid commitments. For example, the UK committed to increase ODA to 0.7 per cent of its gross national income by 2013.

As with Norway's initiative, the idea was that writing off debt would reduce the secondary purchase of debt by commercial creditors and hence reduce the number of lawsuits by vulture fund creditors.

But achieving this depends on the G8 countries fulfilling their promises and on the HIPC countries meeting the conditions imposed by the IMF and the World Bank.

8.4 The Paris Club Initiative (2007)

The Paris Club[84] is an informal group of creditor countries which aim to make co-ordinated efforts towards helping sovereign debtor countries with debt repayment difficulties. Paris Club creditors have collectively agreed to take part in the debt rescheduling process.

Although the Paris Club is not a legal entity, the creditors usually agree on the basis of a number of rules and principles. They operate under the principle of 'comparability of treatment' and believe that no creditor should be regarded as inherently privileged. The creditors agree to participate in rescheduling a HIPC country's debt to respond to a situation of imminent default. The debtor country in turn has to comply with the conditions through an IMF programme. Paris Club creditors make an exception, however, in allowing the indebted country to service their obligations to multilateral creditors such as the IMF and the World Bank first.

Even since the launch of the HIPC Initiative, some Paris Club bilateral creditors have sold their debts to commercial creditors and this has increased the number of lawsuits brought against sovereign debtors. By the end of 2006, 46 lawsuits had been brought against 12 HIPC countries, in which the courts had awarded judgment for a total sum of US$1.2bn.[85] In 2007, the Paris Club issued a statement calling on its members not to sell their debts to creditors who were unwilling to participate in the debt relief programme.

> **Paris Club statement**
>
> The Paris Club[86] has expressed its concern about aggressive litigation against HIPCs and has adopted several practical measures to tackle it. In a press release dated 22 May 2007, the group expressed concern about the actions of litigating creditors, as they freeride on the debt cancellation granted by other creditors and thus divert resources from poverty reduction expenditure by the debtor country.
>
> Paris Club creditors also recalled that they are committed to the full implementation of the HIPC Initiative. They urged all official and commercial creditors and debtor countries to take the steps necessary to implement this Initiative. In particular, consistent with the Paris Club principle of comparability of treatment, and taking stock of the harmful consequences of litigation for HIPCs, Paris Club creditors have confirmed that they are committed to avoid selling their claims on HIPCs to other creditors who do not intend to provide debt relief under the HIPC Initiative, and have urged other creditors to follow suit. This call for enhanced co-operative action was reiterated in the Paris Club contribution to the Doha Conference on Financing for Development held in 2008.

8.5 China (2007)

China is committed to providing debt relief to most African countries, although its debt relief programme differs from that of the developed countries and the IFIs. China is not a member of the Paris Club and has not bound itself to the conditions set out in the HIPC Initiatives.

According to the 2007 IMF report,[87] China has agreed to write off all interest-free government loans to HIPC countries that were overdue at the end of 2004. All such debt relief should have been concluded by the end of 2007. As a non-Paris Club bilateral creditor, China also has claims on most post-completion HIPC countries, a total of 20 countries out of 22. It has already signed debt relief agreements with 17 countries. Even though proper statistics are unavailable, the IMF estimates that China has delivered nearly 50 per cent of its share of HIPC Initiative debt relief.[88]

8.6 Jubilee Debt Campaign

The Jubilee Debt Campaign has been instrumental in creating the international will to write off debt problems in developing countries. It has also named and shamed vulture fund creditors during or after litigation. It has pressed for the UK Parliament to pass a law to tackle vulture fund lawsuits in the UK courts.

The campaign has its roots in Jubilee 2000, which campaigned for the cancellation of poor country debt. It came into being as the Jubilee Debt Campaign in March 2001. It is based on the support of millions of individuals worldwide.[89] Its strength lies in the campaigning activities described on its webpage:

> *By uniting our voices, we have forced world leaders to face up to the scandal of poor country debt. With your help, we can force them to end it.*

The Jubilee Debt Campaign's activities have been acknowledged by the UK Government and its campaign has spread to other countries, including the USA.

Conclusion

This chapter has shown that many countries have recognised the need for greater debt relief to help HIPCs. It also shows the need to prevent bilateral creditors from selling their claims on to vulture funds.

Its key lessons are:

- Stopping the sale of unpaid debts through writing off debts should continue;
- The World Bank DRF measures allow creditors to obtain a fair amount of their unpaid debt;
- Implementing the HIPC Initiatives and MDRI is beneficial to countries if they have proper control and if programmes are accountable;
- Campaigns can be successful in situations where moral pressure is required;
- Concerted effort by the international community is necessary to allow indebted countries to achieve the MDGs.

Further reading

- IMF, spring and end of year meetings, http://www.imf.org/
- Jubilee Debt Campaign, http://www.jubileedebtcampaign.org.uk/

CHAPTER 9

Ways Forward

Like slavery and apartheid, poverty is not natural. It is man-made and it can be overcome and eradicated by the actions of human beings.

Nelson Mandela, former South African president,
speaking in support of the Make Poverty History campaign

In September 2000, building upon a decade of major United Nations conferences and summits, world leaders came together at the UN headquarters in New York to adopt the UN Millennium Declaration. World leaders committed their nations to a new global partnership to reduce extreme poverty. They set out a series of time-bound targets, with a deadline of 2015, that become known as the Millennium Development Goals. Whilst there has been considerable success in addressing the problems of unsustainable debt, vulture funds have so far been equally successful in hindering poor countries' progress towards the MDGs. The past decade has been marked by significant changes in debt restructuring patterns, each apparently better than the previous one (see Chapter 8, International Initiatives). But debt restructuring has been less successful than expected.

To tackle the obstructive actions of vulture funds, it is important to note again that debt problems are inextricably linked to the political, economic and social factors prevailing in both creditor and debtor countries. Legislative efforts by the Belgian, UK and other governments demonstrate the need for strong political will to tackle the problem of unsustainable debt and its consequences.

This chapter highlights further solutions which call for new, far-reaching reforms to deal with the problem of unsustainable debt and lawsuits, with a view to controlling vulture fund activities, albeit indirectly.

The proposed solutions discussed here are:

- An international framework to restructure sovereign debt
- An international arbitration court
- A regulatory framework for public financial management

9.1 International framework for restructuring sovereign debt

Debt restructuring has taken different forms as outlined in Chapter 2, Loan Agreements, and Chapter 5, Debt Management. The Baker and Brady Plans were proposed in the 1980s and 1990s. The IMF introduced the HIPC Initiatives of 1996 and 1999 and the Multilateral Debt Relief Initiative in 2005. At present the Debt Reduction Facility is helping control debt reduction and has had positive outcomes.

In 2003, a solution to allow orderly debt restructuring known as the Sovereign Debt Restructuring Mechanism (SDRM)[90] was proposed. Countries facing huge debts start restructuring very late, to the detriment of both the sovereign debtor and its creditors. The SDRM sets out an orderly structure for debt restructuring. It provides for a majority of creditors to reach an agreement that is binding on all the other creditors involved. This mechanism would automatically stop creditors from opting out and litigating against sovereign debtors. In addition, it provides greater safeguards for creditors so they can feel that their interests are protected.

However, the proposal faces strong opposition and has not yet been launched. Its strongest opponent has been the investor community. The belief is that this mechanism will limit creditors' rights and will hamper the efforts of sovereign debtors to repay their debts. In addition, it is argued that the SDRM is incomplete in that it does not cover debts owed to the IMF or other multilateral institutions.[91]

The SDRM appears to have lost credibility with the acceptance of CACs. In addition, it is thought that its implementation may increase the cost of borrowing. The proposed role of the IMF as a 'bankruptcy court' is thought to infringe the principle of neutrality as it would give the IMF conflicting roles as creditor and arbiter.

It is argued that a proper framework for orderly debt restructuring would provide a solution to the problem of hold-out creditors and the rush to court when sovereign debtors fail to repay. However, the framework should be comprehensive and should treat all players in the financial market equitably.

9.2 International arbitration court

At present lawsuits take place in different jurisdictions. For vulture fund creditors, this may not be a problem as they can afford reputable and costly law firms. But sovereign debtors may find it difficult, in terms of both capital and human resources, to represent themselves in court. Whilst some sovereign debtors opt for arbitration, they face the same difficulties.

Arbitration is an alternative method of resolving a dispute outside the traditional court system. It is argued that this will be to the advantage of the sovereign debtor if the debt proceedings are heard before an international arbitration court or tribunal that is a centralised and specialised body with expertise which the indebted countries lack. There are several reasons to opt for this mechanism. It is envisaged that an international arbitration court would employ similar processes in all debt disputes and provide consistency. In the international courts, debtors feel they have unequal power: this would be avoided before an arbitration court. An arbitration court would hold a more neutral position. Unlike judges, arbitrators would not be bound by their countries' policies; they would be experts in related matters and would also look at social, economic and cultural factors.

It is argued that such a court should be established by an international treaty after a study of existing conventions and treaties, under the United Nations Commission on International Trade Law (UNCITRAL) model. Not only should treaties on arbitration and recognition of foreign judgments be considered, but also economic and social rights.

Basically, the method proposed here will involve international bodies and states. An international convention or treaty will need to be agreed and an international arbitration court set up under the treaty. In order to be bound by and subject to the court, countries will need to ratify the treaty.

Again, this is a measure which involves consultation at many levels; consequently it may be a long time before an end result is finally achieved.

9.3 Regulatory framework for public financial management

A regulatory framework for public financial management is seen as one way to deal with the problems of poverty, poor debt management and the damaging lawsuits suffered by HIPC countries. This means the creation of an international debt framework that sets out codes and standards for managing public debt and the relationships between sovereign debtors and their creditors. It is believed that such a framework will create a more predictable situation and help prevent crises. If a crisis does arise, then the framework will also provide an appropriate solution and course of action.

The Legal Debt Clinic considered the speech made by Gordon Brown, then UK Chancellor of the Exchequer, at the 2002 IMF Spring meeting (see box below).[92]

The Clinic carried out a survey of many Commonwealth countries to identify their needs. The responses showed that most of the HIPC countries have very outdated laws pertaining to debt management and borrowing. There has been no regulation of governments' fiscal and monetary policies although it is arguable that there is a strong link between the strength of a government's fiscal and monetary policy and its external debt. In order to achieve high levels of growth and economic stability, a stable fiscal and monetary policy is necessary. In 1996 New Zealand became the first country to pass a Fiscal Responsibility Act, with the aim of bringing its budget deficit under control.

> **Strengthening the international financial system**
>
> *In a world of ever more rapid financial flows, we know that capital is more likely to move to environments which are stable and least likely to stay in environments which are, or become, unstable. And we know that countries who need capital most are, at the same time, the most vulnerable to the judgments and instabilities of global financial markets. So for every country, rich or poor, macroeconomic stability is not an option but an essential precondition of economic success. ... It is in the interests of stability – and of preventing crises in developing and emerging market countries – that we seek a new rules-based system, under which each country, rich and poor, has a responsibility to adopt agreed codes and standards for fiscal and monetary policy for the financial sector and for corporate governance. This adoption of clear transparent procedures would improve macroeconomic stability, deter corruption, provide to markets a flow of specific country by country information that will engender greater investor confidence and reduce the problem of contagion. ... And where countries do operate transparent and effective systems, fully monitored by the international community, they have the right to expect the support of the international community if hit by financial contagion.*
>
> Gordon Brown, UK Chancellor of the Exchequer, 2002

In April 2008 the Legal Debt Clinic presented a document proposing a fiscal responsibility framework to HIPC finance ministers at the Commonwealth Ministerial Debt Sustainability Forum Meeting in Washington.[93] In July 2008, the same proposal was presented to Commonwealth law ministers at their meeting in Edinburgh, Scotland.[94] At the time the Clinic was making this proposal, Nigeria was the only African country to have passed a Fiscal Responsibility Act.

Whatever the law is called, a fiscal responsibility framework should follow five basic principles. These are:

- Transparency in the setting of fiscal policy objectives, the implementation of fiscal policy and the publication of the public accounts;

- Stability in the fiscal policy-making process and in the way fiscal policy impacts on the economy;

- Responsibility in the management of the public finances;

- Fairness, including between generations; and

- Efficiency in the design and implementation of fiscal policy and in managing both sides of the public sector balance sheet.

The main characteristics of proper public debt management – transparency, accountability and reporting mechanisms – were almost non-existent in most of the countries included in the needs assessment conducted by the Legal Debt Clinic.

The lack of legal measures setting out transparency, accountability and reporting requirements in many countries has allowed them to suffer from the profligate attitudes of their governments. A fiscal responsibility law framework adapted to each country's needs is the most appropriate way in which indebted countries can tackle this problem.

On the other hand, most of the Francophone indebted countries have passed a basic common regulation regarding such a framework. It appears that this has helped some of the western Francophone countries to pave the way for stability in their economies. The indebted Commonwealth countries may need to work together to develop a similar framework incorporating the principles set out above.

Following the financial crisis of 2008, the UK Government concluded that legislation to ensure accountability and transparency was needed as never before. It passed the Fiscal Responsibility Act in February 2010, creating a legal requirement to secure sound public finances and placing a binding duty on the government to implement it. By legislating for fiscal responsibility, the UK Government aimed to halve the budget deficit, as noted in the Queen's speech in 2009:[95]

> My Government's overriding priority is to ensure sustained growth to deliver a fair and prosperous economy for families and businesses, as the British economy recovers from the global economic downturn. Through active employment and training programmes, restructuring the financial sector, strengthening the national infrastructure and providing responsible investment, my Government will foster growth and employment.
>
> As the economic recovery is established, my Government will reduce the budget deficit and ensure that national debt is on a sustainable path. Legislation will be brought forward to halve the deficit.

The Legal Debt Clinic supports the setting up of a robust framework for fiscal responsibility, with mechanisms for accountability, transparency and reporting. An appropriate institutional set-up dealing with debt management should operate within such a framework to ensure the correct economic strategy in the long term to achieve sustainable debt. The Clinic advocates an international regulatory framework for public financial management comprising the concepts of fiscal responsibility, appropriate codes of conduct for borrowing, settling loan repayments and regulating both borrowers and lenders.

Conclusion

The three proposed solutions discussed in this chapter – an international framework to restructure sovereign debt, an international arbitration court and a regulatory infrastructure for public financial management – go beyond the operations of vulture funds and deal with wider reforms to deal with the problems of sovereign debt.

The lessons to apply here are:

- International reforms are needed to deal with vulture fund lawsuits; these are not simply a domestic issue for a sovereign country.

- A more regularised and focused method of dispute resolution will cause less harm to sovereign countries and their economies. It will also avoid unnecessary costs, huge legal fees and unknown legal principles.

- On the national level, better regulation of fiscal policies with greater transparency, reporting and accountability will help effective debt management.

- The financial crisis of 2008 and the Asian crisis of 1997 should be analysed to learn lessons about how to avoid unsustainable debts and lawsuits.

- All the institutions involved must assume responsibility, including donors, sovereign debtors, commercial creditors and international financial institutions. There needs to be responsible borrowing, but also responsible lending. Only a code of conduct can regulate these matters

Further reading

- 'Fiscal Responsibility Laws – More Popular Than Ever Thanks to the Crisis', posted by Holger van Eden, available at http://blog-pfm.imf.org/pfmblog/2009/08/fiscal-responsibility-laws-more-popular-than-ever-thanks-to-the-crisis.html, accessed on 24 May 2010

- Model Fiscal Responsibility Framework, available at http://www.thecommonwealth.org/document/181889/34293/35232/181429/clmm2008.htm

- Report to Commonwealth Finance Ministers on Work done by the Legal Debt Clinic, at http://www.thecommonwealth.org/files/202185/FileName/CommonwealthSecretariatlegaldebtclinicApril09.ppt, accessed on 20 March 2010.

CHAPTER 10
Conclusion

Where's their conscience? What do they say as a conscience? They don't care?

President Ellen Johnson Sirleaf of Liberia

This Handbook has shown the importance of understanding the nature of vulture fund operations and lawsuits. It has highlighted the need to persist with practical action, vigilance and capacity building, and the potential for wider solutions, especially legislation.

To date, claims under lawsuits that have already been lodged are estimated to be worth US$1.5bn; a total of 54 creditors have lodged cases. In 2007, US$1.2bn was awarded by the courts. The number of lawsuits may increase, as there are many commercial loans which have not been resolved in Liberia, Côte d'Ivoire and Central African Republic. However, while no recorded lawsuits were lodged in any court in 2008, there was no such success in 2009, when Liberia, Argentina and DR Congo faced legal action by their creditors.

Vulture fund lawsuits have hampered the progress of debt relief in vulnerable poor countries, as this Handbook shows. However, at international level there is a formidable consensus that unsustainable debt must be resolved and eradicated. Though the process of debt relief has been slow and the HIPC Initiatives have not been completely successful, the actions of the G8, Norway and China are highly commendable. Similarly, Belgium's action in legislating to protect sovereign debtors against the actions of vulture funds has given an impetus to positive change. The recent UK legislation will bring about a reduction in the amount claimed and obtained by vulture funds and this may force them either not to lodge cases in the UK or to negotiate and obtain out of court settlements for one year. It is hoped that the Bill introduced in the USA will eventually become law. If debt relief programmes succeed, the countries concerned will be set on the path of debt sustainability. In addition, if these countries can establish a clear procedural framework for borrowing and debt management, coupled with the necessary accountability and transparency, this will pave the way to greater economic stability and further sustainable development in the long run.

It is strongly argued on the basis of the evidence contained in this Handbook that the way forward lies in basic principles of law and legislation. Technical and advisory assistance or financial support towards legal costs cannot on their own eradicate vulture fund lawsuits. The only way in which vulture funds can be tackled is by legislation such as that passed by Belgium and the UK and under consideration in the USA.

In the absence of such legislation, campaigns such as those waged by the Jubilee Debt Campaign and other NGOs will continue to raise awareness and exert moral pressure. G8 country initiatives in writing off debts have helped in the recent financial crisis, which would have been even more of an uphill struggle without them. Ironically, however, after the financial crisis of 2008, the advanced economies are facing their own debt crises, with the challenge of reducing debt loads which could hamper their economic growth.

When vulture funds target the assets of a sovereign debtor, they hold the country to ransom. In the case of Liberia, where the vulture funds Hamsah Investments and Wall Capital Ltd obtained a judgment for US$20m in November 2009, the funds opted to sue in order to reap the benefits of debt relief monies. It does not matter to the funds that Liberia has been plagued by war for decades and is one of the poorest countries in the world. A sovereign country is advised always to resist the claims of vulture fund creditors on moral grounds.

In defence of unethical vulture fund activities, the financial world argues that vulture fund operations are necessary for the smooth functioning of the secondary debt market. However, looking at the results of attachment orders and garnishee orders against a sovereign debtor in the cases brought against DR Congo, it is not clear how they have served this aim. Most vulture funds have been created specifically to buy one or two sovereign distressed debts and little is known about them, while reputable hedge funds and commercial creditors have co-operated in writing off debts or in the buy-back processes.

It can be argued that there are natural obligations under a loan agreement – that the sovereign debtor has an obligation to pay and the creditor a right to obtain payment. The Commonwealth Secretariat Legal Debt Clinic argues that people have a fundamental right to dignity and a decent life. Many people in the indebted countries live on less than a dollar a day, and the action of the vulture funds in taking away debt relief monies is a breach of this fundamental human right.

This brings us back to our introduction. The question that arises is whether the principles of legal egalitarianism should apply when the sovereign debtor is a country in debt distress, and where poverty and hunger prevail. Should concerned parties react differently when action is being taken to alleviate poverty and prevent the situation worsening in hard times? The simple answer is yes, we should react differently as it is a matter of an overriding human right. The Legal Debt Clinic hopes that such an argument will be forcefully presented in future court cases where the actions of vulture funds are eroding the benefits of debt relief. It hopes too that a responsible attitude to both lending and borrowing, a transparent and accountable debt framework with effective reporting mechanisms, and the efforts of the international financial community will open the way to greater stability and economic justice.

Notes

1. Debt Relief (Developing Countries) Act 2010 (see Annex 3 of this Handbook).
2. Quoted by *BBC News*, 15 February 2007, http://news.bbc.co.uk/1/hi/business/6365433.stm
3. http://www.informationclearinghouse.info/article17070.htm
4. *IMF Report*, August 2003, http://www.imf.org/external/pubs/ft/wp/2003/wp03161.pdf
5. http://www.guardian.co.uk/business/2007/oct/17/debt.law
6. 194 F.3d 363 (2nd Cir. 1999).
7. http://www.guardian.co.uk/business/2007/oct/17/debt.law
8. Response to Jubilee Debt Campaign and Oxfam email campaign on vulture fund litigation against Zambia dated 24 June 2007, http://www.hm-treasury.gov.uk/development_vulture fund.htm
9. 'Vulture Fund Threat to Third World', Wednesday, 14 February 2007, http://www.gregpalast.com/vulture-fund-threat-to-third-world/ and 'Palast Hunts the Vultures for BBC', Friday, 26 February 2010, http://www.gregpalast.com/palast-hunts-the-vultures-for-bbc/
10. 109 F.3d 850. 65 USLW 2640 (2nd Cir. 1997).
11. [2007] EWHC 197 (Comm).
12. 'Vulture Fund Threat to Third World', Wednesday, 14 February 2007, http://www.gregpalast.com/vulture-fund-threat-to-third-world/
13. http://www.afdb.org/fileadmin/uploads/afdb/Documents/Legal-Documents/30774810-EN-NEW-GENERAL-CONDITIONS-ADB-SOVEREIGN.PDF, accessed on 12 March 2010.
14. [2007] EWHC 197 (Comm).
15. See case law mentioned in Chapter 3, Lawsuits (note 29).
16. [2007] EWHC 197 (Comm), paragraphs 10–12. Author's italics.
17. http://www.opsi.gov.uk/RevisedStatutes/Acts/ukpga/1978/cukpga_19780033_en_1
18. http://ednet.rvc.cc.il.us/~PeterR/IR/docs/fsia.htm
19. CACV 373/2008 & CACV 43/2009.
20. 676 F.2d 47 (2nd Cir. 1982).
21. 504 U.S. 607 (2nd Cir. 1992)
22. 159 U.S. 113 (1895) reported at paragraph 16 of judgment of *Pravin Banker Associates Ltd v Banco Popular del Peru and the Republic of Peru* (1997).
23. 109 F.3d 850. 65 USLW 2640 (2nd Cir. 1997).
24. Paragraph 17 of judgment.
25. [1996] 3 All ER 431.
26. 194 F.3d 363 (2nd Cir 1999).
27. [2007] EWHC 197 (Comm).
28. [2007] EWCA Civ 148.
29. *Elliott Associates, LP* General Docket No 2000/QR/92 (Court of Appeals of Brussels, 8th Chamber, 26 September 2000).
30. 194 F.3d 363 (2nd Cir. 1999).
31. *Elliott Associates v Republic of Peru*, 12 F. Supp. 2d 328 (S.D.N.Y. 1998).
32. *Elliott Associates, LP* General Docket No 2000/QR/92 (Court of Appeals of Brussels, 8th Chamber, 26 September 2000).
33. *Kensington International Ltd v Republic of the Congo* [2003] EWCA Civ 709.
34. *FG Hemisphere Associates, LLC v DR Congo* 455 F. 3d 575 (5th Cir. 2006).

35 455 F. 3d 575 (5th Cir. 2006).
36 [2007] EWCA Civ 148.
37 [2007] EWCA Civ 148.
38 [2007] EWHC 197 (Comm).
39 [2007] EWHC 197 (Comm).
40 Paragraph 501 of judgment.
41 Paragraph 167 of judgment.
42 Paragraph 186 of judgment.
43 Paragraph 409 of judgment.
44 *Kensington International Ltd v Republic of the Congo* [2005] EWHC 2684 (Comm).
45 Civil Case Nos. 03-1314 (RJL) 03-1315 (RJL) at https://ecf.dcd.uscourts.gov/cgi-bin/show_public_doc?2003cv1315-63
46 www.karrass.com
47 http://www.liberianobserver.com/node/3194, accessed on 20 March 2010.
48 [2007] EWHC 197 (Comm).
49 IMF and World Bank, 'Guidelines for Public Debt Management', http://siteresources.worldbank.org/INTDEBTDEPT/Resources/PDMGuidelines20031209.pdf
50 http://web.worldbank.org/WBSITE/EXTERNAL/TOPICS/EXTDEBTDEPT/0,,contentMDK:21289856~menuPK:4876257~pagePK:64166689~piPK:64166646~theSitePK:469043,00.html
51 http://blogs.cgdev.org/globaldevelopment/2009/04/liberia-cuts-its-debt-with-12-billion-buy-back-at-97-percent-discount.php, accessed on 19 March 2010.
52 http://treasury.worldbank.org/bdm/htm/guidelines_publicdebt.html, accessed on 19 March 2010.
53 [2007] EWHC 197 (Comm).
54 'Heavily Indebted Poor Countries (HIPC) Initiative and Multilateral Debt Relief Initiative (MDRI) – Status of Implementation', 12 September 2008, Paragraph 40, http://www.imf.org/external/np/pp/2007/eng/082807.pdf
55 [2007] EWCA Civ 148.
56 Debt Relief (Developing Country) Act in UK and Stop Vulture Funds Bill in USA.
57 Charlotte Denis, 'Retreat by Nestlé on Ethiopia's $6 Million Debt', 20 December 2002, at http://www.guardian.co.uk/world/2002/dec/20/marketingandpr.debtrelief, accessed on 18 March 2010.
58 http://icsid.worldbank.org/ICSID/FrontServlet, accessed on 19 March 2010.
59 'Big Food Group Backs Down on $12 Million Compensation from Guyana', *Business Respect*, 17 March 2003, at http://www.businessrespect.net/page.php?Story_ID=869, accessed on 18 March 2010.
60 http://www.imf.org/external/np/pp/2007/eng/082807.pdf, paragraph 48, accessed on 18 March 2010.
61 http://www.imf.org/external/np/pp/2007/eng/082807.pdf, paragraph 47, accessed on 18 March 2010.
62 http://www.thecommonwealth.org/Shared_ASP_Files/UploadedFiles/4FF51600-BF54-44A8-BDFA-525A2C5768CC_cfmm2006-finalcommunique(2).pdf, accessed on 19 March 2010.
63 http://www.thecommonwealth.org/files/182536/FileName/FINAL-LMM-COMMUNIQUE.pdf, accessed on 19 March 2010.
64 http://www.imf.org/external/np/pp/eng/2008/091208.pdf
65 http://www.afdb.org/en/news-events/article/african-legal-support-facility-constitutive-assembly-takes-place-in-tunis-4808/

66. http://www.mconnartymp.com/michael-connarty-mp-urges-support-for-vulture-funds-bill.html, accessed on 19 March 2010.
67. James Moore, 'Time to Clip the Wings of the Vultures', *The Independent*, 28 November 2009, http://www.independent.co.uk/news/business/analysis-and-features/time-to-clip-the-wings-of-the-vultures-1830037.html, accessed on 20 March 2010).
68. http://www.lachambre.be/kvvcr/showpage.cfm?section=none&language=fr&leftmenu=none&cfm=/site/wwwcfm/flwb/FlwbChronology.cfm?sdocname=52K0762&id=018523&legislat=52&inst=K&dossierID=0762&db=FLWB, accessed on 20 March 2010.
69. Foreword, 'Consultation Paper on Vulture Funds', July 2009, p. 3, at http://www.hm-treasury.gov.uk/d/consult_effectivedebtrelief_200709.pdf, accessed on 20 April 2010.
70. http://www.hm-treasury.gov.uk/d/consult_effectivedebtrelief_200709.pdf, accessed on 20 March 2010.
71. http://edmi.parliament.uk/EDMi/EDMDetails.aspx?EDMID=38604&SESSION=899
72. http://www.hm-treasury.gov.uk/d/consult_effectivedebtrelief_response_190210.pdf, accessed on 20 March 2010.
73. http://www.hm-treasury.gov.uk/development_action_vulturefunds_article.htm, accessed on 20 March 2010.
74. www.opsi.gov.uk/acts/acts2010/pdf/ukpga_20100022_en.pdf
75. http://www.epolitix.com/latestnews/article-detail/newsarticle/sally-keeble-mp-regulating-vulture-funds/
76. http://www.govtrack.us/congress/bill.xpd?bill=h110-6796, accessed on 20 March 2010.
77. http://www.opencongress.org/bill/111-h2932/, accessed on 20 March 2010.
78. http://www.opencongress.org/bill/111-h2932/, accessed on 20 March 2010.
79. IMF Factsheet, June 2009.
80. http://web.worldbank.org/WBSITE/EXTERNAL/TOPICS/EXTDEBTDEPT/0,,contentMDK:21288373~pagePK:64166689~piPK:64166646~theSitePK:469043,00.html, accessed on 21 March 2010.
81. *Towards the Year 2000 and Beyond: The Norwegian Debt Relief Strategy*, www.norway.org/News/archive/2001/200103debt.htm
82. http://www.norway.az/policy/humanitarian/figures/debtreliefplan.htm
83. Gleneagles Communiqué, 2005.
84. http://www.clubdeparis.org/en/
85. http://ec.europa.eu/development/body/tmp_docs/2007/2007_HIPC.pdf, accessed on 21 March 2010.
86. http://www.clubdeparis.org/sections/themes-strategiques/2009-8217-action-du-club, accessed on 21 March 2010.
87. http://www.imf.org/external/np/pp/2007/eng/091007.pdf
88. Ibid.
89. http://www.jubileedebtcampaign.org.uk/?lid=123, accessed on 21 March 2010.
90. http://www.imf.org/external/np/exr/facts/sdrm.htm
91. http://www.imf.org/external/np/pdr/sdrm/2002/112702.htm
92. http://www.imf.org/external/spring/2002/imfc/stm/eng/gbr.htm, accessed on 21 March 2010.
93. http://www.thecommonwealth.org/files/202185/FileName/CommonwealthSecretariatlegaldebtclinicApril09.ppt, accessed on 11 March 2010.
94. http://www.thecommonwealth.org/Internal/190714/190927/157583/160518/reports/ and http://www.thecommonwealth.org/files/202185/FileName/CommonwealthSecretariatlegaldebtclinicApril09.ppt, accessed on 20 March 2010.
95. http://www.number10.gov.uk/Page21351, accessed on 22 March 2010.

Bibliography

African Forum and Network on Debt and Development (AFRODAD), 'Fair and Transparent Arbitration on Debt', Issues paper No. 1/2002, January 2002.

Arewa, Olufunmilayo B, 'Vultures, Hyenas, and African Debt: Private Equity and Zambia', *Northwestern Journal of International Law and Business*, 2009.

Bradlow, Daniel D, 'Some Lessons About the Negotiating Dynamics in International Debt Transactions', UNITAR Discussion Document No. 9, 2000.

Caribbean Financial Advisory Services Ltd and Nathanson, Nabarro, 'Dealing with Sovereign Debt in Distress: Some Key Financial and Legal Aspects', *Commonwealth Law Bulletin*, 30, 2004.

Gathii, James Thuo, 'Sanctity of Sovereign Loan Contracts and Its Origins in Enforcement Litigation', *George Washington International Law Review*, 2006.

Hagan, Sean, 'Designing a Legal Framework to Restructure Sovereign Debt', *Georgetown Journal of International Law*, Winter 2005.

Häseler, Sönke, 'Individual Enforcement Rights in International Sovereign Bonds', Institute of Law and Economics, University of Hamburg, 10 November 2008.

Herbert, Carla. 'Designing a Legal and Regulatory Framework for Better Public Financial Management: Some Issues for Consideration from Trinidad and Tobago', *Commonwealth Law Bulletin*, 33 (2 & 3).

HM Treasury (2009). 'Ensuring Effective Debt Relief for Poor Countries: A Consultation on Legislation', July 2009.

IMF, 'The Logic of Debt Relief for the Poorest Countries', IMF paper, September 2000, available at http://www.imf.org/external/np/exr/ib/2000/092300.htm

IMF, 'Debt Relief Under the Heavily Indebted Poor Countries Initiative', IMF Factsheet, June 2009.

IMF and World Bank, Statement by the Hon. Gordon Brown, Governor of the Fund for the UK at the Joint Annual Discussion, Board of Governors, 2002, Press Release No. 66, 29 September 2002, Washington DC.

Jessee, Janna, 'Gleneagles G8 Commitments on Debt Relief and Aid – Two Years On', House of Commons Library Research Paper 07/51, 4 June 2007.

Jones, Meirion, 'Vulture Fund Threat to Third World – How Corporations Continue to Rape the World's Poor', BBC, *Newsnight*, 14 February 2007, available at http://www.informationclearinghouse.info/article17070.htm

Jubilee USA Network, 'Vulture Funds: Compromising the Gains of Debt Cancellation', available at http://www.jubileeusa.org/fileadmin/user_upload/Resources/vulturefundpolicybrief0507.pdf, accessed on 13 May 2010

Keeble, Sally, 'Regulating Vulture Funds', 6 May 2009, available at http://www.epolitix.com/latestnews/article-detail/newsarticle/sally-keeble-mp-regulating-vulture-funds/

Kopits, George. 'Fiscal Rules: Useful Policy Framework or Unnecessary Ornament?', IMF Working Paper, WP/01/145, 2006.Mai, Chiang, 'Improving Global Governance for Development: Issues and Instruments', Thailand, 8–10 December 2002.

Pessoa, Mario, 'Promoting Fiscal Discipline – Fiscal Responsibility Laws', 28 December 2007, available at http://blog-pfm.imf.org/pfmblog/2007/12/promoting-fisca.html, accessed on 13 May 2010.

Raffer, Kunibert, 'Which Sovereign Debt Workout Arrangements? Proposing a Model for Meaningful Debt Relief', EU-LDC Conference, 2002.

Reisen, Helmut, 'Is China Actually Helping Improve Debt Sustainability in Africa?', Preliminary draft for International Conference on 'Emerging Powers in Global Governance', 6–7 July 2007.

'Resolving Sovereign Debt Crises with Collective Actions Clauses', *FRBSF Economic Letter*, No. 2004–06, 20 February 2004

Salmon, Felix, 'In Defense of Vulture Funds', 24 February 2007, http://www.felixsalmon.com/000667.html, accessed on 20 March 2010.

Schmerler, Charles D, 'Creditors No Longer Hesitate to Go to Court, and the Debate Now Centers on Enforcement', *New York Law Journal*, 22 February 2005.

'Stop Vulture Culture', Trans Africa Forum, Justice for the African World available at http://www.jubileeusa.org/fileadmin/user_upload/Resources/Vulture_Funds/Vulture_Funds_TAF_7_09.doc

Stewart, Heather, 'Vulture Fund Swoops on Congo Over $100m Debt', *Observer*, 9 August 2009.

UNCTAD, 'Vulture funds, Moral Issue or Real Threat?', Debt Management Conference, 20 November 2007.

Vásquez, Ian, 'The Brady Plan and Market Based Solutions to Debt Crises', *The Cato Journal*, No. 16, Vol. 2, http://www.cato.org/pubs/journal/cj16n2-4.html

Websites

Commonwealth Secretariat, Legal Debt Clinic website, http://www.thecommonwealth.org/Internal/190714/190927/157583/legal_debt_clinic/

Greg Palast's featured documents and videos on vulture funds, at http://www.gregpalast.com

Jubilee Debt Campaign, http://www.jubileedebtcampaign.org.uk/

World Bank website on Debt Relief and the HIPC Initiative, http://web.worldbank.org, accessed on 20 March 2010.

List of Cases

Barbados Trust Co Ltd v Bank of Zambia [2007] EWCA Civ 148

Booker plc v Co-operative Republic of Guyana (ICSID Case No. ARB/01/9)

Camdex International Ltd v Bank of Zambia [1996] 3 All ER 431

Donegal International Ltd v Republic of Zambia & Anor [2007] EWHC 197 (Comm)

Elliott Associates, LP General Docket No 2000/QR/92 (Court of Appeals of Brussels, 8th Chamber, 26th Sept 2000)

Elliott Associates, LP v Banco de la Nacion and The Republic of Peru 194 F.3d 363 (2nd Cir. 1999)

Elliott Associates v Republic of Peru, 12 F. Supp. 2d 328 (S.D.N.Y. 1998)

FG Hemisphere Associates, LLC v Democratic Republic of the Congo & China Railway Groups and Ors CACV 373/2008 & CACV 43/2009

FG Hemisphere v DR Congo Civil Case Nos. 03–1314 (RJL) 03–1315 (RJL)

FG Hemisphere Associates, LLC v The République du Congo 455 F. 3d 575 (5th Cir. 2006)

Hilton v Guyot 159 U.S. 113 (1895)

Kensington International Ltd v Republic of the Congo [2005] EWHC 2684 (Comm)

Libra Bank Ltd v Banco Nacional de Costa Rica 676 F.2d 47 (2nd Cir. 1982)

Pravin Banker Associates Ltd v Banco Popular Del Peru and the Republic of Peru 109 F.3d 850. 65 USLW 2640 (2nd Cir. 1997)

Republic of Argentina v Weltover 504 U.S. 607 (2nd Cir. 1992)

Annex 1

US Court Judgment in *FG Hemisphere Associates, LLC v Democratic Republic of Congo and Société Nationale D'Électricité (S.N.E.L.)*

UNITED STATES DISTRICT COURT
FOR THE DISTRICT OF COLUMBIA

FG HEMISPHERE ASSOCIATES, LLC,	)	
Plaintiff,	)	
v	)	
DEMOCRATIC REPUBLIC OF CONGO,	)	Civil Case Nos. 03-1314 (RJL)
and SOCIETE NATIONALE	)	03-1315 (RJL)
D'ELECTRICITE (S.N.E.L.),	)	
Defendants	)	

MEMORANDUM ORDER
(March 19, 2009) [#102]

Presently before the Court is plaintiff's Motion for a Civil-Contempt Order and Sanctions against defendant the Democratic Republic of Congo ("DRC") in these consolidated actions.[1] Because DRC has failed to comply with this Court's prior discovery orders, the Court will GRANT plaintiff's motion in part.

On September 28, 2006, this Court granted plaintiff's September 29, 2005 Motion to Compel [Dkt. #74] by Minute Order, stating:

> It is hereby ORDERED that defendant the Democratic Republic of the Congo must conduct and complete a diligent, good faith search, both inside and outside the United States, for all documents responsive to Plaintiff's First Requests for Production, as modified by Plaintiff's letter of September 7, 2005, within thirty days from the date of this Order; and Defendant must certify that such a search has been conducted, describe with specificity the steps undertaken, and provide all responsive, non-privileged documents it has located to plaintiff, together with a certification that it has produced all such documents, within thirty days from the date of this Order.

---

[1] For reference purposes, all docket numbers identified herein refer to the docket numbers in Case No. 03-1314 (RJL).

(Minute Order, Sept. 28, 2006). Subsequently, by agreement of the parties, on November 28, 2006, the Court imposed a bifurcated discovery plan and stayed DRC's obligations under the September 28, 2006 Minute Order pending completion of Phase I of the plan.[2] (Order, Nov. 28, 2006 [Dkt. #88].) Upon completion of Phase I, and again by agreement of the parties, on February 12, 2007 the Court ordered completion of Phase II of the plan, ordering that DRC

> shall have ninety (90) days from the date of this Order in which to respond to plaintiff's discovery requests related to discovery in aid of execution of the default judgments with respect to properties outside the territorial jurisdiction of this Court, including the discovery compelled pursuant to the Court's September 28, 2006 Order.

(Order, Feb. 12, 2007 [Dkt. #93].) DRC thereafter served on plaintiff a Certification of Efforts and Responses to Requests for Production on May 14, 2007 and filed a notice with the Court the next day certifying its compliance with the Court's February 12, 2007 and November 28, 2006 Orders.[3] (DRC's Notice of Compliance, May 15, 2009 [Dkt. #99].)

DRC's discovery response, however, fell woefully short of compliance. DRC did not produce *any* documents pertaining to DRC assets "outside the territorial jurisdiction of this Court," but rather, re-produced duplicates of documents pertaining to DRC's Washington, DC assets that were subject to Phase I of the discovery plan. DRC also failed to provide the required certification that a search occurred for the Phase II documents and that all responsive, non-privileged documents were produced, Indeed, DRC concedes as much in its response to plaintiff's motion, arguing not that it complied with the Court's discovery orders, but rather that sanctions would be futile. (Def.'s Response at 2-4 [Dkt #103].

Accordingly, upon consideration of plaintiff's Motion for a Civil-Contempt Order and Sanctions, DRC's opposition thereto, oral argument held March 6, 2009, and the entire record herein, it is hereby

---

[2]Phase I of the bifurcated discovery plan focused "on discovery in aid of execution against any property belonging to defendant Democratic Republic of Congo within the territorial jurisdiction of this Court." (Order, Nov. 28, 2006.) In that phase plaintiff sought "discovery designed to determine whether any such properties exist that may be immune from execution under the Foreign Sovereign Immunities Act." (*Id.*)

[3]In the interim, on March 13, 2007, DRC filed an appeal of this Court's November 9, 2006 Minute Orders denying defendants' Motions to Vacate the Default Judgments. (Notice of Appeal, Mar. 13, 2000 [Dkt. #96].) Coinciding with its appeal, DRC filed a motion to stay its discovery obligations, which this Court denied. (Minute Order, May 1, 2007.)

ORDERED that, pursuant to the Court's inherent power to enforce compliance with its orders, *Armstrong v. Executive Office of the President, Office of Admin.*, 1 F.3d 1274, 1289 (D.C. Cir. 1993), and based on plaintiff's clear showing that DRC violated this Court's unambiguous discovery orders of February 12, 2007 and November 28, 2006, DRC is in CIVIL CONTEMPT; and it is further

ORDERED that DRC, within 30 days from the date of this Order, shall:

(1) conduct and complete a diligent good-faith search for all documents concerning its assets outside the District of Columbia pursuant to the terms of this Court's prior discovery orders; and

(2) certify that it conducted such a search, describe with specificity the steps it took in conducting that search, and provide to plaintiff all responsive, non-privileged documents it has located, together with a certification that it has produced all such documents; it is further

ORDERED that if DRC fails to complete the aforementioned search and production within 30 days from the date of this order, DRC shall show cause on or before the expiration of the 30-day period why a fine payable to plaintiff should not be imposed in the amount of $5000 per week, doubling every four weeks until reaching a maximum of $80,000 per week, until DRC satisfies its discovery obligations under this Order. In the event DRC fails to complete the search and production, plaintiff shall have 14 days after the earlier of the expiration of the 30-day period or DRC's show-cause filing in which to file a response; it is further

ORDERED that, pursuant to Fed. R. Civ. Pro. 37(b)(2), DRC shall pay to plaintiff the reasonable expenses, including attorney's fees, plaintiff incurred in making this motion, as well as all other costs and expenses incurred by plaintiff that were caused by DRC's failure to comply with the Court's Orders of February 12, 2007 and November 28, 2006. Plaintiff shall file with this Court and serve DRC through counsel an itemized listing of all such costs and expenses it wishes to claim within 30 days from the date of this Order. DRC shall become liable to pay plaintiff the full amount set forth within 20 days from the date of such filing, unless it files an objection in writing to particular items or amounts and makes application to this Court to disallow any such items or amounts. Prior to making such application, the parties shall meet and confer in good faith in an effort to resolve any disputes by agreement.

SO ORDERED.

RICHARD J. LEON
United States District Judge

Annex 2

Belgian Legislation

PROPOSITION DE LOI

Article 1ᵉʳ

La présente loi règle une matière visée à l'article 78 de la Constitution.

Art. 2

Les sommes destinées à la coopération au développement ou à l'aide au développement, octroyées à des États ou à des organismes étrangers ayant obtenu la garantie de leur gouvernement, de leur banque centrale ou d'une institution qui exécute la politique de développement d'un État étranger, sont insaisissables et incessibles.

Les montants des prêts consentis à des États ou à des organismes étrangers ayant obtenu la garantie de leur gouvernement, de leur banque centrale ou d'une institution qui exécute la politique de développement d'un État étranger, comme prévu à l'article 5 de la loi du 3 juin 1964 modifiant l'arrêté royal n° 42 du 31 août 1939 réorganisant l'Office national du Ducroire et autorisant le ministre des Finances et le ministre qui a les Relations commerciales extérieures dans ses attributions, à consentir des prêts à des États ou à des organismes étrangers, modifié par l'arrêté royal n° 75 du 10 novembre 1967 modifiant la loi du 3 juin 1964, sont insaisissables et incessibles.

Art. 3

La présente loi entre en vigueur le jour de sa publication au *Moniteur belge*.

12 décembre 2007.

PROPOSED LAW[1]

Article 1

The present law is made under Art 78 of the Constitution[2].

Article 2

The funds given towards the development and cooperation or to help towards developing infrastructures given, to sovereign states or foreign corporations which have obtained the guarantee from their government, or the central bank or any institution which executes the policy of development of foreign sovereign states, **cannot be seized nor transferred.** The amount of aid given to States or foreign corporations which have obtained the guarantee of their government, of their central bank or any institution which executes the policy of development of foreign sovereign states, as provided in Art 5 of the law of 3 June 1964 modifying the royal decree No 42 of 31 August 1939 reorganising the National Office of Ducroire and authorising the Minister of Finance and the Minister of Foreign Commerce Relations in its functions, to give loans to sovereign states or foreign corporations as modified by the royal decree No 75 of 10 Nov 1967 modifying the law of 3 June 1964, **cannot be seized nor transferred**.

Article 3

The present law comes into force on the day of its publication in the Belgian 'Moniteur'[3]

---

[1]Translation done by the author.
[2]Article 78 of the Constitution provides the medium through which a law is passed. Draft bills are adopted by the Chamber of Representatives and are then forwarded to the Senate.
[3]On 31st Jan 2008, the Belgian Senate unanimously approved the resolution and the law.

Annex 3

The UK Debt Relief (Developing Countries) Act 2010

CHAPTER 22

CONTENTS

Introduction

1 Meaning of "qualifying debt" etc

2 Qualifying debts: further definitions

Relief of debts etc

3 Amount recoverable in respect of claim for qualifying debt etc

4 Meaning of "the relevant proportion"

5 Judgments for qualifying debts etc

Supplementary and general

6 Exception where debtor fails to make offer to pay recoverable amount

7 Exception for overriding EU or international obligations

8 Saving

9 Duration of Act

10 Commencement, extent and short title

Debt Relief (Developing Countries) Act 2010

2010 CHAPTER 22

Make provision for or in connection with the relief of debts of certain developing countries. [8th April 2010]

BE IT ENACTED by the Queen's most Excellent Majesty, by and with the advice and consent of the Lords Spiritual and Temporal, and Commons, in this present Parliament assembled, and by the authority of the same, as follows: –

Introduction

1 Meaning of "qualifying debt" etc

(1) This section applies for the purposes of this Act.

(2) "The Initiative" means the enhanced Heavily Indebted Poor Countries Initiative of the International Monetary Fund and the World Bank.

(3) "Qualifying debt" means a debt incurred before commencement that –

(a) is public or publicly guaranteed,

(b) is external,

(c) is a debt of a country to which the Initiative applies or a potentially eligible Initiative country, and

(d) in the case of a debt of a country to which the Initiative applies, is incurred before decision point is reached in respect of the country.

(4) For the purposes of subsection (3) treat a debt incurred after commencement as incurred before commencement if (and so far as) it replaces one incurred before commencement.

(5) For the purposes of subsection (3)(d) treat a debt incurred after decision point as incurred before decision point if (and so far as) it replaces one incurred before decision point.

(6) "Potentially eligible Initiative country" means a country –

(a) that the International Monetary Fund and World Bank identify as potentially eligible for debt relief under the Initiative, and

(b) in respect of which decision point has not been reached.

(7) Decision point is regarded as reached in respect of a country if it is so regarded for the purposes of the Initiative.

(8) For the meaning of other expressions used in subsection (3), see section 2.

(9) "Country" includes a territory.

(10) "Commencement" means the commencement of this Act.

(11) If the terms of the Initiative are amended after commencement in such a way as to change a relevant eligibility condition, this Act has effect as if they had not been so amended.

(12) In subsection (11) "relevant eligibility condition" means a condition as to the level of a country's income or debt or the size of its economy that must be met in order for the country to be eligible for debt relief under the Initiative.

2 Qualifying debts: further definitions

(1) The expressions used in section 1(3) have the meaning given below.

(2) "Debt" includes—

(a) a liability that falls to be discharged otherwise than by the making of a payment,

(b) an obligation to repurchase property that arises under an agreement for the sale and repurchase of property (whether or not the same property), and

(c) a liability of the lessee under a finance lease (except a liability so far as relating to the operation or maintenance of property subject to the lease).

(3) "Debt" does not include —

(a) a liability to pay for goods or services that arose on the delivery of the goods or the provision of services,

(b) a liability that falls to be discharged in less than a year from the time it was incurred ("a short-term debt") unless the short-term debt is within subsection (4), or

(c) a liability incurred after commencement that replaces anything that was (at the time of the replacement) within paragraph (a) or (b).

(4) A short-term debt is within this subsection if it ought to have been discharged –

(a) more than a year before commencement, and

(b) (where decision point has been reached in respect of the country concerned) more than a year before decision point.

(5) A debt is a "public" debt of a country if it was incurred by–

(a) the country or any part of it (or the government of the country or any part of the country or any department of any such government),

(b) the central bank or other monetary authority of the country, or Debt Relief (Developing Countries) Act 2010 (c. 22) 3

(c) a body corporate controlled (directly or indirectly) by anything within paragraph (a) or (b).

(6) In subsection (5)(a) references to part of a country include any municipality or other local government area in the country.

(7) A debt is a "publicly guaranteed" debt of a country if –

(a) it is guaranteed,

(b) the guarantee was entered into –

(i) before commencement, and

(ii) where decision point has been reached in respect of the country, before that point was reached, and

(c) the debt would be a public debt of the country if it had been incurred by the guarantor.

(8) If the conditions in subsection (7)(a) to (c) are met as regards part of a debt, that part is regarded as a publicly guaranteed debt of the country concerned.

(9) A public or publicly guaranteed debt of a country is "external" unless the creditor was resident in the country –

(a) if decision point was reached in respect of the country before commencement, at the time that point was reached, or

(b) otherwise, at commencement.

(10) If in any proceedings there is an issue as to whether a debt is a qualifying debt, treat the debt as external unless it is proved in those proceedings that it is not external.

Relief of debts etc

3 Amount recoverable in respect of claim for qualifying debt etc

(1) The amount recoverable in respect of —

    (a) a qualifying debt, or

    (b) any cause of action relating to a qualifying debt, is the relevant proportion of the amount that would otherwise be recoverable in respect of the qualifying debt or cause of action.

(2) For the meaning of "the relevant proportion", see section 4.

(3) Subsection (1) does not apply in relation to an agreement (a "compromise agreement") that compromises—

    (a) a claim for a qualifying debt, or

    (b) a claim in respect of a cause of action relating to a qualifying debt.

(4) But the amount recoverable under a compromise agreement is limited to the amount that would be recoverable in respect of the claim if the agreement had not been made (and subsection (1) applied to the claim).

(5) Subsection (1) does not apply where an agreement that is not a compromise agreement (a "refinancing agreement") has been made—

    (a) that changes the terms for repayment of a debt ("the rescheduled debt") in such a way as to reduce its net present value, or

    (b) by virtue of which a debt ("the original debt") is replaced by a debt ("the new debt") whose net present value is less than the net present value of the original debt.

(6) But the amount recoverable in respect of the rescheduled debt or the new debt is limited to the amount that would be recoverable in respect of the initial debt if the refinancing agreement had not been made (and subsection (1) applied to that debt).

(7) In subsection (6) "the initial debt" means the debt mentioned in subsection (5)(a) or (as the case may be) the original debt.

(8) References in this section to the amount recoverable include the amount recoverable on the enforcement of any security.

(9) This section applies even if the law applicable to the qualifying debt, or to any compromise agreement, refinancing agreement or security, is the law of a country outside the United Kingdom.

4   **Meaning of "the relevant proportion"**

(1) In this Act any reference to the relevant proportion, in relation to a qualifying debt, is to be read as follows.

(2) Where the qualifying debt is one to which the Initiative applies, the relevant proportion is –

$$\frac{A}{B}$$

where –

A is the amount the debt would be if it were reduced in accordance with the Initiative (on the assumption, if it is not the case, that completion point has been reached, for the purposes of the Initiative, in respect of the country whose debt it is), and

B is the amount of the debt without it having been so reduced.

(3) Where the qualifying debt is a debt of a potentially eligible Initiative country, the relevant proportion is 33%.

5   **Judgments for qualifying debts etc**

(1) This section applies to –

   (a) a judgment on a relevant claim given by a court in the United Kingdom before commencement,

   (b) a foreign judgment given (whether before or after commencement) on a relevant claim, and

   (c) an award made (whether before or after commencement) on a relevant claim in an arbitration (conducted under any laws).

(2) "Relevant claim" means –

   (a) a claim for, or relating to, a qualifying debt, or

   (b) a claim under an agreement compromising a claim within paragraph (a).

(3) The amount of the judgment or award is to be treated as equal to the amount it would be if the court, tribunal or arbitrator had applied section 3 in relation to the relevant claim.

(4) Subsection (3) does not apply in relation to a claim if the effect of it so applying would be to increase the amount of the judgment or award.

(5) In this section —

"judgment" includes an order (and references to the giving of a judgment are to be read accordingly), and

"foreign judgment" means a judgment (however described) of a court or tribunal of a country outside the United Kingdom, and includes anything (other than an arbitration award) which is enforceable as if it were such a judgment.

(6) This section applies to anything that gives effect to a compromise of a relevant claim as if in subsection (3) after "if" there were inserted "the relevant claim had not been compromised and".

Supplementary and general

6 Exception where debtor fails to make offer to pay recoverable amount

(1) This Act does not apply to a relevant claim, a relevant foreign judgment or a relevant arbitration award if —

(a) proceedings are brought in respect of the relevant claim, foreign judgment or arbitration award, and

(b) the debtor does not, before the relevant time, make an offer to compromise the proceedings on comparable Initiative terms.

(2) For the purposes of this section an offer is made on "comparable Initiative terms" if the net present value of payments to be made in accordance with the offer is equal to or exceeds the net present value of the payment required to satisfy the relevant claim, foreign judgment or arbitration award (reduced in accordance with this Act).

(3) In this section—

"foreign judgment" has the meaning given by section 5(5),

"judgment" includes an order,

"proceedings" means proceedings in a part of the United Kingdom, and includes proceedings for—

(a) the registration of a foreign judgment or an arbitration award, or

(b) permission to enforce an arbitration award in the same manner as a judgment of the court,

but does not include proceedings for the enforcement of a judgment or award, "relevant arbitration award" means an award within section 5(1)(c),

"relevant claim" has the meaning given by section 5(2),

"relevant foreign judgment" means a foreign judgment within section 5(1)(b), and

"the relevant time" means—

(a) the time when a court first gives judgment on the relevant claim, Debt Relief (Developing Countries) Act 2010 (c. 22)6

(b) the time when the foreign judgment or arbitration award is registered, or (as the case may be)

(c) the time when permission is given to enforce the arbitration award in the same manner as a judgment of the court.

(4) This section applies to cases where the proceedings were brought before commencement (as well as cases where they are brought after commencement), but not to cases where the relevant time occurred before commencement.

7 Exception for overriding EU or international obligations

(1) Nothing in this Act applies to a foreign judgment or an arbitration award of a kind required by European Union law, or by an international obligation of the United Kingdom, to be enforced in full even in cases where such enforcement is contrary to the public policy of the United Kingdom.

(2) Accordingly, this Act does not apply to —

(a) a foreign judgment that is certified as a European Enforcement Order (within the meaning of Regulation (EU) No. 805/2004 of the European Parliament and of the Council),

(b) a foreign judgment that is an enforceable European Order for Payment (within the meaning of Regulation (EU) No. 1896/2006 of the European Parliament and of the Council), or

(c) an award to which section 1 of the Arbitration (International Investment Disputes) Act 1966 applies (awards made under the Convention on the settlement of investment disputes between States and nationals of other States).

(3) "Foreign judgment" has the meaning given by section 5(5).

8 Saving

Nothing in this Act enables a person to recover anything paid in (total or partial) satisfaction of any liability (whether arising under an agreement, judgment, order, award or otherwise).

9 Duration of Act

(1) This Act expires at the end of the period of one year beginning with commencement; but this is subject to subsections (2) and (3).

(2) The Treasury may by order provide that this Act (instead of expiring at the time it would otherwise expire) expires at the end of the period of one year from that time.

(3) The Treasury may by order provide that this Act has permanent effect.

(4) An order under this section is to be made by statutory instrument.

(5) An order under this section may be made only if a draft of the statutory instrument containing it has been laid before, and approved by a resolution of, each House of Parliament.

(6) If this Act expires by virtue of this section—

(a) the Act is to be treated as never having been in force, and

(b) accordingly, where —

(i) a judgment was given, or order or arbitration award made, on a relevant claim (as defined by section 5(2)) while the Act was in force, and

(ii) the amount of the judgment, order or award is, as a result of section 3, less than it would be if that section had not applied in relation to the claim,

the amount of the judgment, order or award is to be treated as equal to the amount it would be if the section had not applied in relation to the claim.

10 Commencement, extent and short title

(1) This Act comes into force at the end of the period of two months beginning with the day on which it is passed.

(2) This Act extends to each part of the United Kingdom.

(3) This Act may be cited as the Debt Relief (Developing Countries) Act 2010.